The Direct
Ceremonies
and
Assistant Director of Ceremonies

Richard Johnson

Lewis Masonic

The Director of Ceremonies
Richard Johnson

First published 2010

ISBN 978 085318 347 1

© Richard Johnson 2010

Published by Lewis Masonic
an imprint of Ian Allan Publishing Ltd, Hersham, Surrey KT12 4RG.
Printed in England by Ian Allan Printing Ltd, Hersham, Surrey KT12 4RG.

Visit the Ian Allan Publishing website at www.ianallanpublishing.com
Distributed in the United States of America and Canada by BookMasters Distribution Services.

Contents

Foreword

I have great pleasure in writing a short foreword to this interesting and instructive book by W.Bro. Richard Johnson, PPrSGD of the Province of Cumberland and Westmorland.

Bro. Johnson has fulfilled the requirements for a good and reliable Guide Book for Directors of Ceremonies and those interested in this important office.

Custom and practice varies from lodge to lodge but the subjects covered in this book will be helpful to all readers.

I anticipate that this Guide Book will open the eyes of readers to the hidden mysteries of the work of the Director of Ceremonies and I commend Bro. Johnson for his enthusiastic work.

Norman James Thompson
Provincial Grand Master
Cumberland and Westmorland

Acknowledgements

I would like to thank the several lodges that allowed me to browse through their records of different aspects of the ceremonies performed. I would like to express my appreciation of the constructive comments on the text made by Chris Godden of Nourse Lodge 8590 (now sadly passed to the Grand Lodge Above), and also Norman Thompson of Huddleston Lodge 6041, and Trevor Phillips of Lodge of Unanimity 113 for proofreading the book; as well as placing on record – as ever – the patience of my wife Linda while I was immersed in researching and compiling this book.

The publishing royalties from this book will be donated to the Province of Cumberland and Westmorland's 2016 Festival for the Royal Masonic Benevolent Institution (RMBI).

Preface

It was in 1844 that Alexandre Dumas wrote a book called *The Three Musketeers*. In it were detailed some of the adventures of Athos, Porthos and Aramis, who enjoyed somewhat exalted status in the French Court in the 1620s, and their meeting and befriending of a young newcomer called D'Artagnan, who by joining in some of their exploits was eventually accepted by them and made the trio into a quartet.

So what has this to do with a Masonic lodge? Certainly not the swordsmanship and several other aspects of the lives of these seventeenth-century heroes, but they carried out the private orders of the King and Queen of France, and organised themselves to deliver what was required and within the desired timescale. In the same way it could be said that the Secretary, Director of Ceremonies and Treasurer are the main organisers or components of the 'engine room' of any lodge, each often staying in post for several years which gives a useful continuity to lodge operations. D'Artagnan in this case might represent the Master of the lodge, a newcomer to this elevated status (unless the lodge is recycling Past Masters), who is eager to be guided by those with more experience but who may also have quite firm ideas of his own on what could and should be done during his year.

This book forms part of a series concerned with assisting brethren who have taken on different offices within their lodges, the previous books having covered the duties of the Assistant Officers and then the Principal Officers – i.e. the conventional ladder to the Chair of the lodge. Here we concentrate on the role of the Director of Ceremonies, leaving the role of the Secretary and the Treasurer for separate volumes. For the Director of Ceremonies particularly, there will be aspects of his duties that have been partly covered in the advice for the other lodge Officers, and to avoid laboured repetition between the books these aspects have not all been reiterated verbatim in this volume.

Those who that have been in post for several years will be performing many of the jobs routinely and to the satisfaction of the lodge members – otherwise they would not still be in office, so perhaps this book may be of interest to them essentially as an *aide-mémoire*. It has been written, however, mainly for the benefit of the brother who is thinking about or has been invited to become the next Director of Ceremonies or his assistant, or someone who is thinking of volunteering for the job, and who wishes to learn something about the extent of his new duties. He will eventually be helpfully briefed by his predecessor before any hand-over of responsibilities occurs, but often it is valuable to be able to absorb quietly some general practical advice and guidance even before that briefing. Then he will have a preliminary awareness of what will be required, and he can use the briefing to elicit additional information on any remaining areas of concern.

At his investiture, the main duties of the Director of Ceremonies are outlined simply in his address as seeing that 'the ceremonies are carried out correctly, all attendees are seated according to status, and the Officers are in place'. Rarely can so much responsibility be covered by only 19 words. He thus oversees the physical running of the meetings and practices, and covers all aspects of each participant knowing exactly what to do and when and where. His jurisdiction remains solely within the confines of the lodge, and he only has contact with the outside world when dignitaries come to visit.

So to move away from the swashbuckling activities of the seventeenth century, perhaps a more modern analogy for the roles of the engine room individuals within the lodge might be found in clubs playing association or rugby football. The Secretary and Treasurer will be looking after the administration and financial affairs of the club, while the Director of Ceremonies is more like the team coach – ensuring that each of the players is at peak fitness and totally aware of the appropriate tactics and set pieces for every game. And like a team coach, his role is not to be gesticulating at his players wildly from the sidelines, but to ensure that the team participants in every game (or lodge meeting) will be the ones receiving all of the plaudits from the visitors.

And it is useful to remember that the lodge has requested you personally to undertake the office. It does not expect you to be a perfect clone of the previous incumbent; indeed it might be hoped that in some ways you perform your duties a little differently, so you do not have to follow exactly the same style as your predecessor. Indeed life would be the poorer if there were no differences between us all, just as one of the pleasures of visiting lodges is to see how each copes with essentially the same Masonic business in a variety of ways. So do not be afraid to bring your own charisma to the job in hand; usefully adopt the best attributes of the person before you, and introduce some new ideas to other aspects of the office, and you will be able to strike an effective balance between continuity and a new broom.

It should be noted that in this book there are repeated references to 'Province' and 'Group'. I am aware that collections of lodges overseas are called 'Districts' and are largely equivalent to the UK Provinces, and that some Provinces use the terminology 'District' instead of 'Group' for a collection of lodges in one locality or under one Assistant Provincial Grand Master for example. It would be appreciated if the reader could bear this in mind if his region adopts one of the other titular options, but this request seems preferable to using Province/District and Group/District throughout and where the different interpretations of 'District' may cause confusion. The relatively recent creation of the first Metropolitan Grand Lodge as the London equivalent of a Province, rather than remaining under the direct jurisdiction of the Grand Master, has also served to circumvent the requirement to constantly insert the London equivalent to Provincial protocol where appropriate. Where there are some specific differences between the operations of the District and Metropolitan Grand Lodges and the Provincial Grand Lodges, these are usually commented on as appropriate.

Introduction

"I keep six honest serving-men
(They taught me all I knew);
Their names are What and Why and When
And How and Where and Who."

Rudyard Kipling, Just So Stories (1902),
The Elephant's Child

Rudyard Kipling's listing of his serving-men, "What and Why and When and How and Where and Who", is perhaps applicable to both the Secretary and the Director of Ceremonies alike. For the Director of Ceremonies, with regard to all of the ceremonies that he will be trying to organise throughout the year, he will need to know what ceremony is being worked, when it will be performed, the lodge traditions for how exactly it will be conducted and whereabouts in the lodge room and by whom. From the junior members in particular, he will doubtless be inundated with questions as to why the different parts of the ceremony are performed in these ways, what significance they have, and historically how they arose, and so on.

It has already been said that the Director of Ceremonies is somewhat like a team coach, always in full control of whatever is happening, but operating and encouraging largely in the background. The team squad has discussed and talked through the game plan at length, and during the game the coach might have to resort to one or two signals or even brief verbal instructions/reminders – in American football some team players have microphones and speakers in their helmets so that a private word can suffice, but as yet neither English association or rugby football club players wear such helmets, and neither normally do Masons in lodges, so sometimes the communications will have to be visible and audible to all those present.

The Director of Ceremonies is an 'additional' lodge officer and not mandatory, but despite this, few lodges choose to manage without one. The Director of Ceremonies operates within the precincts of the lodge, and he ensures that everything that happens in a lodge meeting and at the subsequent meal is performed exactly as it should be. This means he has to be able to maintain the traditions required by the lodge, but also has to ensure that the meetings conform to the expectations of the Masonic hierarchy. This will include the Province in which the lodge resides as well as the more local Group requirements, because from time to time there will be external visitors who will report back if they see anything that they deem to be untoward.

On being invested, the Director of Ceremonies is informed that he is required to see that all of the ceremonies are properly conducted, that visitors and brethren are placed as befits their rank, and that the lodge Officers are situated correctly around the lodge room – and this includes the temporary substitutes if any Officers are not able to be present. In addition to these aspects, we might first assess what characteristics could be useful in a Director of Ceremonies.

Personal Attributes

It is probable that you have already aspired to this office before the lodge has asked you to consider taking it on; this is certainly not an office that should be forced on anyone against his own inclination. You will have a reasonable understanding of the Craft ceremonies, and will undoubtedly have taken part in aspects of each of them; in fact you will have probably progressed through a series of offices within the lodge.

You are probably a Past Master of this or another lodge and, in holding that office, you will already have interacted closely with your own Director of Ceremonies. You will possibly have thought to yourself what an excellent support he was during your year in the Chair. So think about the qualities in him that you admired, and check yourself for similar ones; this is another case of the Wardens' address at the installation: "What you find praiseworthy in others, you should carefully imitate, and what in them may appear defective, you should in yourselves amend." There is nothing wrong in copying role models, because as the head of the Sony Corporation once said about the 'Walkman' portable cassette player clones: "Imitation is the sincerest form of flattery."

But enough of quotes. It will be useful if you are a Past Master, because otherwise you will miss the inner workings of the installation ceremony, and this is just one of the occasions that is likely to run more smoothly with you shepherding things along. You will also be reasonably proficient in the lodge ritual, because this will give you the confidence to advise others, whether by prompting when appropriate or in guiding someone along his own learning path. There is much to be said for being able to lead from the front and being able to deliver all of the ceremonies as required without much warning, and such inherent capability will enable you to go about your duties confidently, but it is not all that is required in this job. I remain unconvinced that the Director of Ceremonies needs to be the best ritualist in the lodge *per se*, just as the best football managers and coaches have not necessarily been the top international players in the earlier stages of their careers.

You will require a clear speaking voice. While a whispering Director of Ceremonies can operate adequately in some lodges, a modicum of extra volume will assist in persuading the brethren to quieten down and to listen to you. And it is surprising how quickly the human voice can be absorbed in a lodge room or at the festive board. The bodies, clothes, and the furnishings such as the carpets, seats, banners and other wall coverings, etc., can make a human voice unheard beyond surprisingly short distances. This is not to say you need a Sergeant Major's stentorian capability, but some volume certainly. And clarity is required at any volume, as well as being able to speak at a controlled pace, rather than being word-perfect and gabbling through your announcement so that no-one is any the wiser as to what you were trying to say. You will have seen many brethren delivering parts of the ritual and other items in different ways, from the excellent to the less so, and you will therefore know what works well and otherwise.

Just as your speaking style may well be an example for the brethren to copy, your standard of dress should also set the standard for the lodge; the white gloves should be clean and the black shoes clean and polished – and preferably avoid using the first to polish the second! Your overall appearance should be tidy, so if formerly you enjoyed a 'wild man of Borneo' style of haircut and attire, you may want to change things. Your appearance will set the tone for other members of the lodge, and will also leave a lasting impression on the dignitaries that will visit the lodge, at installations for example. Remember the warning given to candidates for job interviews – the first impression registered by the interviewers across the table is approximately 7 seconds, i.e. while you are walking from the door to your seat, and before you have even said hello. From that time onwards the meeting is conducted in the minds of the interviewers by them listening and probing with their own questions, and deciding whether they should modify that first impression positively or negatively. Thus a bad first impression can be an insurmountable obstacle to winning the job, even if technically you may be superior to the other applicants.

And you will need to have a degree of dexterity, because you need to make carrying your wand look as if it were born in your hand, and it will be with you for almost everything except when leading the salutations. It is useful if you have a naturally erect posture (remember that you were told as an Entered Apprentice to stand perfectly erect), as you need a confident if not necessarily a commanding stature when you move around the lodge room. That is not to say you should convey a forbidding presence, but rather by your own calm dignity you will be able to inspire calmness and confidence in those you escort; for some junior members perhaps performing their first pieces of ritual inside a full lodge room such inspiration will be most welcome. If the Director of Ceremonies appears to be in control of the situation, even when merely walking across the room to escort someone, it can become infectious by reassuring others and instilling confidence into them. Also unflappability certainly helps when awkward situations arise, such as the Master splitting his trousers at an elevating moment in the third degree, as has occurred more than once during my observations of the ceremonies.

However, perhaps more important than being personally able and skilled in the lodge ritual, you will need to be someone who can work with people. The lodge has made you the Director of Ceremonies in order to preserve the lodge traditions, not by you performing every aspect faultlessly, but by ensuring that every member is fully conversant with the correct way of doing things, from the simplest salutes to the longest pieces of prose. This will require something else from you: time and patience, and to be able to work with and advise others, at the lodge practices and on other occasions, will undoubtedly take a great deal of both.

Before leaving the relevant attributes, it might be worth giving some thought to prompting. It is of course very useful if you as the Director of Ceremonies can immediately produce the perfect prompt at any stage of any ceremony, but even the best of us can be caught out sometimes, and it does not look well for you to be thumbing through or even having an open ritual book on your lap. If you have lots of volunteers around the room, then the prompting from discreetly hidden books can be local to wherever that part of the ceremony is currently taking place. You may delegate the Immediate Past Master to prompt the Master if required; otherwise the Secretary's table is the one place in the lodge room where papers are being spread out and organised for the various communications etc. to be reported, and a prompt sheet or book here would not look out of place. It may be that the Secretary, the Treasurer or the Assistant Secretary can be quietly following the written script, and if for any reason you are temporarily stuck for a prompt, then a quick glance from you across the room should elicit the appropriate response. And the correctness of the assistance is all-important, because a wrong prompt can cause all sorts of confusion in the mind of the recipient, and completely jumble up the rest of the presentation. This is also an argument for only having a single prompt at any time, rather than well-intentioned helpers delivering a variety of different suggestions for the recipient to cope with.

As well as dealing with the pregnant pauses that can occur during the ceremonies, you also have another job which is harder to define. If the delivery of a piece of ritual is not word-perfect, how far off the correct version do you allow it to drift before bringing it back onto the correct track? You will need an appreciation for the importance of what is taking place; perhaps in an obligation there should be less latitude given than in the other parts of the ceremonies. This is a difficult call to make, and as a general rule it is perhaps better to let someone continue in full flow even if he is not 100% accurate. Just as with an incorrect prompt, an interruption can equally cause confusion, and the person delivering the piece of ritual may become disoriented and lose the thread of what he was saying. So you might assess what is important to the candidate, who would clearly benefit from a coherent presentation, and you could correct parts of the obligations as necessary, but allow slight deviations in the explanations of the tracing boards, etc., to go uncorrected if the gist of the story is there and intelligible. It is a personal call, and one you will find useful to try out in the lodge practices as well as in the proper ceremonies, and one you might discuss afterwards with your predecessor. In any event, stay calm and unflappable, trust your instincts, and the lodge will go along with you. Of course, what people do not realise is that, despite the calm exterior, you are probably churning over inside just as much as the more openly nervous people, and you will be fervently hoping that everything goes right.

To assist you in your quest for enlightenment, several Provinces organise workshops for lodge Directors of Ceremonies, not only to outline methods of coping with these kinds of problems, but also to reinforce the Provincial protocol when, for example, receiving dignitaries, so if possible make the most of any opportunities that are presented to you. And it is worth noting that Provincial Directors of Ceremonies do not grow on trees – or indeed have other than normal parentage, but they and their Deputies are gleaned from the lodge equivalents across the Province, so if you have any aspirations in this direction, then the workshops are definitely useful training grounds in order to understand the Provincial protocol *in toto*.

The Lodge Ritual

As Director of Ceremonies, part of your job is concerned with ensuring that each Officer and member understands the lodge ritual. If you are a strict Emulation lodge, then you are fortunate that this is the most common format to be published in books. However, the Nigerian ritual for example is also not far removed from that of Emulation, and lodges using other rituals closely related to Emulation are able to cope by using a standard book plus additional notes. However, in these days of computers and desktop publishing, it is more common for lodges to print their own version of the ritual for their members. Some lodges formally present a master copy of their ritual to a new Director of Ceremonies at his investiture, so that he is fully aware of the nuances that might have escaped his notice while he was an ordinary member. This copy may include additional notes by previous Directors of Ceremonies, as *aide-mémoires* and to further explain various aspects of the ritual in detail.

From time to time the lodge may want to update its ritual. Occasionally Grand Lodge issues edicts about compulsory changes to the wording of the ritual; for example in the 1980s the penalties in the obligations were changed to emphasise their symbolic nature. As Director of Ceremonies you will probably head a small committee of members to discuss and draft revised sections of the current ritual, and a similar exercise will be necessary if you are starting a new lodge and agreeing the ritual to be followed. This committee will probably include the Secretary for any editorial input, although these days you may also have other members with considerable computer, information technology or publishing knowledge and whose experience you can profitably call upon. It is a worthwhile intellectual exercise, as some aspects of the ceremonial you may be assessing in detail for the first time – items that you have never given a second thought to, but another member of the committee may have a different viewpoint, and suddenly the discussion broadens into the historical and other aspects of the lodge and Masonic ritual, and becomes very wide-ranging. It is also an interesting balance, to retain the traditional features of your ritual, while framing it for a lodge that is to operate in the twenty-first century.

Perhaps if you are revising existing ritual, you will report back to the lodge to obtain general acceptance of what the committee has drafted, and then you or the Secretary will obtain quotations for printing books of the final approved text and distribute copies to the members. If you are a new lodge, you may let the ritual settle down by utilising the draft version for the first few years. After all, what seems perfectly reasonable on paper does not always translate into action as envisaged, and there are often minor adjustments to be made after a few trials. You can then finalise any corrections you have made after the practices and ceremonies have been performed, and afterwards go to print.

Man Management
The Director of Ceremonies has usually been appointed because he is seen to be capable of maintaining the lodge traditions, which may include the excellence of the ritual performed, but he should always make the needs of the individual of greater importance. There is surely no point in trying to force someone, clearly struggling with one page of ritual, to have to deliver the six-page charge to a candidate after initiation; sharing out the work should be considered, and try to tailor the task to the capabilities of the individual concerned. If the main aim of the ceremony is for the candidate to learn more about what he has just undergone, does it matter that two or more people deliver the piece of ritual to him? This sharing of the work enables the member with more limited ability to feel he is still contributing positively to the lodge business whilst not over-effacing him.

Undoubtedly it would make the Director of Ceremonies' job very much easier if every Master in turn were a capable ritualist, but if the reverse were the case, should this prevent that member from becoming Master of the lodge? The early designers of the Masonic ritual and the sequencing of Officers were quite astute; the holding of each office from Inner Guard to Senior Warden progressively builds up the capability and confidence of the brother as a training course for being the Master of the lodge. Every credit to those lodges who have and regularly attain high standards in Masonic ritual, and manage to inspire successive Masters to perform well, but in other lodges how many brethren have been put off ever starting to progress towards the Chair of King Solomon by being told that they will have to be able to conduct all three degree ceremonies and the installation ceremony as a basic requirement of being Master? After all, the brethren of the lodge will collectively vote to appoint a Master Elect, and by doing so will be confirming their support for the person they have elected; to assist him in his year as Master, perhaps sharing out the work, may be one of the ways in which they can demonstrate that support.

Encouragement is the key to success. Even from being little boys, each of us has usually responded positively to praise and negatively to criticism, and some things do not change as you grow older. As you successfully achieve one goal, you automatically readjust your sights to higher attainments and, if you have been pleasantly surprised by what you have managed to achieve, you will want to keep surprising yourself. By doing so, you are also complying with the request levelled at you in the charge after your initiation: "endeavour to make a daily advancement in Masonic knowledge." So the person who starts out with perhaps somewhat limited capabilities can with time and encouragement develop into being able to perform the required ritual satisfactorily. He may not actually enjoy the work it entails because it does not come naturally to him, but he will achieve a quiet satisfaction of a job done to the best of his abilities, probably surpassing his own expectations at the outset, and perhaps even yours.

What Each Officer Wants from You
You will know that any ceremony is a team effort, from the Tyler preparing the candidate, the Inner Guard admitting him, the Deacons escorting him, the Wardens questioning him, and the Master obligating him, and perhaps others joining with additional aspects of the ceremony. It is obvious that you cannot personally carry out every role, and you have to entrust most if not all aspects of the ceremony to the appointed Officers or their stand-ins. So what advice will be most helpful to them? This is where you need to know each person as an individual; his strengths, his weaknesses, and his overall capabilities – this is one reason why the Director of Ceremonies is usually someone who has been a member of the lodge for a considerable time, so that he knows and is known by all of the members.

Probably the first advice for each Officer is to read the whole ceremony thoroughly in his ritual book, concentrating on the times when he is interacting with the candidate and other Officers. He needs to know the words correctly, and also know the questions or answers that follow in the various colloquies, and that in themselves prompt a further interchange. He will also be aware that whatever he says has to be audible, usually to everyone in the room, sometimes as a stage whisper to the candidate, and therefore he needs to enunciate clearly in order to be understood. Although those who are not used to public speaking may find it difficult at first, a slow delivery of words will be more easily heard than a rapid-fire one, especially as the furnishings of lodge rooms tend to absorb the human voice and can sometimes reduce the different parts of a sentence to a single almost amorphous entity.

The Officers will also need to know what actions are required and when, because parts of the ceremonies have a visual impact as well as an audible one, on both the candidate and other attendees. Equally importantly to the Officers is to be reminded how the lodge copes with those less formal parts of the meetings outside the ceremonies. Each lodge will have its own style of opening and closing, and of performing all of the other items on the agenda, but rarely are they all written down in extensive detail in a ritual book, let alone in an Emulation or other standard version. Possibly the previous incumbent will have made notes to cover these aspects, and he may give you a copy of them to help you along the first few meetings until you have assimilated the role you have taken on.

A *résumé* of the various aspects on which the Officers will probably want advice is given in the Appendix, but the key person who needs your support is the one who appointed you, the Master. For the remainder of his installation meeting and for the bulk of the next lodge meeting, everything is new to him, and yet frequently Directors of Ceremonies do not take sufficient time to go through the whole running agenda of a meeting with a new Master. His copies of the first few summonses are likely to be covered with additional notes, as indeed yours will be to some extent for every meeting, as reminders of what is required and when. With the idea of helping the Master, some lodges seat the Director of Ceremonies next to him, rather than rely solely on the Immediate Past Master, so that there can be quiet words of guidance available throughout the meeting and hopefully they will enable him to cope with every situation.

If other lodge members apart from the Officers are also taking part in the ceremonies, they also will need to know when and where they are required to be. If they are to be escorted it is quite easy – you will take them to where they need to be. If they are to make their own way across the lodge room, then it is also simple – they go to stand in front of the candidate ready to address him. If two or three brethren are delivering an item between them, perhaps one of the tracing boards, then they each make their own way forward in turn to deliver their respective parts, and the only request you may make is that they perhaps sit next to each other, so that it takes on the appearance of well-rehearsed team members each coming off the bench in turn during a game.

Practice Meetings
The best training ground for lodge members to test their memories and capabilities is the lodge practice. Some lodges hold one before each meeting, others may hold two or more (especially before an installation), and it is at these practices that the Director of Ceremonies discovers whether he is heading for a perfect or difficult ceremony at the following lodge meeting. This is also the time to take some corrective action if it looks like the latter, and remember that learning the Masonic ritual takes place in two different spheres of life: firstly the learning is mainly done individually in private, not in public as when reciting the times tables in school. Secondly the choreography of how to arrive at the appropriate place to deliver the next phase of the ceremony is where the public practice has most to offer, when juniors can run through the routine movements and interactions in the lodge – and can take on different roles at each practice, so that they begin to assimilate the flow of the ceremonial in the lodge. If you have candidates or are going to perform a demonstration ceremony at a lodge meeting, then the immediately prior practice is likely to be performed by the same Officers in the practice who will shortly be operating in lodge. To make it more representative of the coming ceremony, you might bring out the lodge regalia to make it a dress rehearsal. Other lodge members can substitute for any Officers that are absent, and this is a useful way of allowing juniors to occupy the vacant posts and gain experience of participating in a ceremony from inside the team rather than merely watching as interested spectators.

If the practice is conducted without any sign of a ritual book, except from where the prompting is to be given, then by attempting to deliver their parts from memory you and the Officers can see how near perfection each of them are. You will all need to agree a signalling system that solicits a prompt only when required. When delivering the charge after initiation for the first time in lodge, at the prior practice I requested a prompt only if I looked round for one; otherwise I would be pausing for breath. At the practice my pauses after each paragraph became longer and longer to emphasise the point, but no prompts were forthcoming as they were not needed. In the lodge meeting the pauses were strictly for breath and shorter in duration than at the practice, but I felt confident that I would not be immediately assailed by a salvo of well-intentioned prompts from around the room at each intake of breath. It is a system that I have seen adopted successfully in many lodges and seems to work well, but there may be other methods that your lodge has found to be suitable for its needs, so use them. Ensure that everyone understands your system, and also that there is only one prompt, from you or the official prompter, rather than a multiplicity of them.

If some members are struggling to cope with their parts, they should perhaps have informed you before the final practice, but what do you do in this situation? After the practice session you might take the Officer to one side and discuss how best to make the necessary improvements. If a Deacon is not sure about the perambulations and positioning the candidate, then let him walk through his steps with you as the candidate a couple of times so that he builds up more confidence about where to be and how to arrive there. If remembering the words is problematical, then check if he has the time to read the different sections again over the next few days, and try to arrange for you or the Assistant Director of Ceremonies or another colleague to visit him at home in order to quickly run through the items again. You might also ask an experienced colleague to sit near the Officer during the lodge meeting, so that there is support nearby if it is required. And often it is remembering the first words of a paragraph that is the problem, and a quiet and timely prompt will trigger the required continuation and would hardly be noticed by others during the ceremony.

In one of my lodges we had a Master who had not found the ritual easy to cope with during his progression through the various offices in the lodge, and wanted an additional practice for his own benefit. The other

Officers who were able to attend met at his house between the two lodge practices, and he went through the parts of the ceremony quietly and with increasing confidence, and in all of his subsequent ceremonies he acquitted himself very well. On these occasions the lodge Director of Ceremonies was never present, as only the junior Officers attended, but I am sure that he was kept up to date on how things were going and would have assisted further if he had thought it necessary.

If you are one of those lodges that holds more than one practice per lodge meeting, then you may call one the junior practice and another the senior practice. The latter has been described above, for the role-players in the coming ceremony, but in the other you have the opportunity to let the youngsters (Masonically at least) try their hands at taking the parts of the lodge Officers. In fact your lodge may have sufficient juniors to hold a Juniors' Night in lodge, although these days Past Masters' Nights generally seem to greatly outnumber the others. You can let some juniors look after some basic elements of the ceremony – the questions and answers of the Wardens and Deacons, and the Inner Guard and Tyler admitting the candidate. The working tools in all three degrees are useful solo exercises, as are the north-east and south-east corner addresses in the first and second degrees, the questions and answers from the Master to the candidate (Deacon) and the charges in the second and third degrees. The obligations should ideally be given as a whole, even the longer first and third degree ones, but the first degree charge may be split into two or more sections. The traditional history and the second degree tracing board explanation can also be split into more sections, and by the time you break down the first degree tracing board or some of the lectures you may have a half dozen or more taking part.

And then a thought comes into your mind – why not let the juniors deliver that first degree tracing board as a team, not just in the practice, but in the lodge as well? If your lodge is blessed with numerous juniors, they will each be several years from the Master's chair, so why not give them something to get their teeth into? If they are a good team, as happened in one of the Preston lodges after the Second World War when they received invitations from other lodges to demonstrate their capabilities, you then have juniors acting as ambassadors of your lodge. Even if you cannot aspire to those levels and operate only within the confines of your own lodge, the short sections of learning that each junior does will be usefully stored away for future reference when his turn comes to go through the Officers' progression to the Master's chair.

All of this organisation takes some planning, and time is something that a Director of Ceremonies requires in no small measure. However, the benefits can be enormous, because now you can see which of the juniors is inspired enough to learn, not just his section, but the next part in the sequence. In my early lodge years I was allocated one part of the first degree charge to learn, and surprising myself that it had not turned out to be too onerous, I learned the next paragraph, and then the next, and relatively soon I had the gist of the whole charge. However, I had never openly tackled more than a couple of sections in the junior practices and had only delivered the second degree working tools formally in lodge, when out of the blue the new Master asked me to deliver the charge to the first initiate in his year. Somebody had been quietly watching my enthusiasm and progress and decided that I could be entrusted with that responsibility, and I have no doubt the Director of Ceremonies and his predecessor at the practices had kept their eyes open for someone willing to put in the required amount of work. And you can benefit similarly, by observing which juniors are keen to learn and are capable of undertaking certain roles if required. It might be that one Officer informs you in good time that he cannot attend the next lodge meeting, and to have some eager and well-rehearsed junior understudies in the wings makes your life a lot easier in such a situation.

You are also able to spot the otherwise enthusiastic members who do not find learning easy, because not everyone is a born ritualist and we all learn at different rates. In their cases they may benefit from some additional tuition, perhaps for a few minutes after the lodge practice, or perhaps in their home if they wish it to be less formal. You will have to decide with your Assistant Director of Ceremonies how to split up this additional work, and you may also reassess the sizes of the chunks of ritual into which you split the ceremonies; you may perhaps select slightly smaller passages for some to cope with, while others can be stretched into tackling longer ones. This is returning to man management, and tailoring the tasks to the capabilities of the different people, so no more needs to be repeated here.

Each of us has his own way of tackling a new item to learn, and the learning of the text is done mostly in private, but you as Director of Ceremonies will be able to advise on different methods if asked, and one such method was outlined in the book for Principal Officers. As a final note, always place the emphasis on encouraging anyone trying to learn a part of the ritual, rather than offering nit-picking and potentially destructive criticism. When the person is trying to deliver his part from memory, perhaps ask for his ritual book; then while he is performing you can mark in pencil where he missed words or put in the wrong ones, and perhaps where he paused or needed a prompt, so that he knows where to concentrate his revision. If the delivery was almost perfect, quietly congratulate him and inform him that he is very nearly there, but if he could make these few changes he would be spot on; the learning was done in private, and perhaps this encouragement should be made individually. And if you have a reputation in the lodge for good ritual, this will be accepted as praise indeed, and will hopefully spur him on to greater things.

Lodges of Instruction
Some lodges have created a Lodge of Instruction. This is a practice organised under another name, but it is run on much more formal lines. The leader is designated the Preceptor, who is often the Director of Ceremonies of the lodge, and it requires formal minutes to be taken and a list of appointed Officers to be kept (Book of Constitutions [BoC] 132-135). It is probable that there will be a schedule of tasks that each member is to undertake in turn, and a record kept of all of the items that he has mastered during his time in the Lodge of Instruction. The whole concept is to develop each Mason so that when he arrives at any rung on the progression of offices towards the Master's chair, he has a thorough grounding in everything he requires in order to do it well. It also spreads out the learning required by the Master for his year of office, because in strict Emulation lodges the Master conducts the whole of each ceremony from start to finish. This is in contrast to other lodges, which in their third degree ceremonies may split the work between the Master and the Immediate Past Master, with the latter delivering the traditional history. Of course, Masters of Emulation lodges have the chance of going to London to demonstrate a degree ceremony after which, if successfully

completed, they are presented with a silver matchbox as a mark of their proven ability – the margins for error are very small, and the award is well merited.

Not every lodge requires a Lodge of Instruction, preferring the more informal way of operating. But for the keen Masons who want to try this more formal type of practice, they will normally be welcome as visitors and will sometimes be allowed to join in, so you may want to ascertain where there are Lodges of Instruction in your area and on which nights they meet. In fact, it will do you no harm to visit yourself because, just as when visiting other lodges you can pick up tips on ways of interpreting the ritual, these formal sessions can provide a useful extension to your experience, and as you probably prefer to see any ritual performed well, you will enjoy watching some enthusiastic youngsters being put through their paces.

Members Losing Enthusiasm
In the course of running many of the practices, perhaps sharing the work with your Assistant Director of Ceremonies, you will sometimes notice members who begin to attend infrequently. Perhaps they are very busy at work, which may take them away from home for extensive parts of the week, or they may have young children to cope with, but you will notice when they start to miss practices without any prior apology. This could be one of the first signs that they are less enthusiastic about the lodge and its ritual than others, and if they fall out of the routine of attending the lodge and practice meetings, it may not be too long before their resignation follows.

The Secretary is able to check lodge attendances from the attendance register, and you and he need to liaise if there is a potential problem developing. The initiate is the star of his first evening, and he is the central focus of his passing and raising ceremonies, but in the larger lodges the wait before he starts on the ladder of lodge offices leading to the Chair may be prolonged. This may be the time to check if he would like to enjoy a fuller role in lodge proceedings, and also to assess if the ceremonies could be broken into smaller parts in order to let some of the juniors participate. Some Provinces recommend that Past Masters perform all of the ceremonial work in the lodge, as a way of keeping them involved after their year in the Chair, but this is less than helpful in encouraging the youngsters to do anything significant.

This may also be the time for you, his proposer or his seconder to talk over with him the progression of offices leading to the Master's chair, and to point out that people develop at their own rate by learning small parts of the ritual before tackling the bigger chunks. If you have a lot of enthusiastic youngsters, then why not have a Juniors' Night in the lodge, and see how they perform? I would wager they will not let themselves or the lodge down, and just watch the renewed interest in attending the practice meetings. If work or family commitments require his attention for some time to come, then ensure he understands that he is welcome at the lodge whenever he is able to attend, and that when the pressures diminish and he is ready to start to participate more actively in the life of the lodge, it will always be ready to assist him in any way it can. We are all members of the Masonic family, and the positive support that a lodge can give any of its members, and not just when they are ill, should never be underestimated or forgotten.

In a similar vein, watch for the Past Masters losing interest in the lodge after they have been Immediate Past Master and Tyler, if the latter office follows the Immediate Past Master. They were in the top echelons of the lodge for several years, pedestals and reserved seats at the meals etc., and suddenly they are not having much to do. You as Director of Ceremonies should ensure that everyone is busy, and if you have several candidates then you might suggest to the Master that each lodge Officer could do one of each of the Craft ceremonies, and then perhaps let someone else take over his role in any repeat ceremonies. If traditionally you already have Juniors' and Past Masters' Nights, then all of the Officers are aware that in some meetings each year they will be replaced, and there will be no potential resentment. If you do not have such traditions, then you might suggest to the Lodge Committee that a very slight change of direction in organising and carrying out the ceremonies may be in the best interests of the lodge and its members; most members will go along with the suggestion to try it and see what reaction is produced. For example, in my lodge an Installing Master was expected to present all of the working tools in full to his successor. One Master approaching the installation hand-over had never delivered the third degree working tools, and I was asked to assist him by delivering them on his behalf (my first time too). Two other juniors asked if they could deliver the second and first degree working tools, and the Past Masters went into a huddle with the Master, who declared that he would in no way be insulted if the lodge removed all of the tool presentations from him on this occasion. Such were the plaudits for the three juniors and congratulations on the obvious good health of the lodge, from the representative to everyone else who was allowed to speak in lodge and at the banquet, that a new lodge tradition was instantly born! So try to take a problem and turn it into an opportunity for the lodge to benefit from.

General Ceremonial

Preparing the Lodge Room

As Director of Ceremonies you will need to arrive early for the lodge meeting in order to check that all is ready for the evening. You may in fact be responsible for preparing the lodge room, or you may have someone else who does that for you – such as the Tyler, but in your particular role you are responsible for everything that happens on the day. As an *aide-mémoire* a checklist of various items to remember is given in the Appendix, but you may find that your lodge has additional items that are required in the different ceremonies, so treat the list as a basis rather than a catch-all.

As well as checking that you are ready for the meeting, try to spot each Officer in turn as he arrives so that you ensure your whole team is present, because you may be approaching a Past Master or two to fill in at short notice for any unforeseen absentees. If it is the first lodge meeting after the installation, then there may be several promoted Officers checking their new bearings, so try to have some time for each of them if required. And if you have substitutes for those Officers who have warned you they will not be there, welcome them as well – especially any juniors you have asked to be in the team temporarily. They will be nervous and may want a few words or a quick revision of some aspects of their duties in order to calm their nerves. If you have a Juniors' Night, then there may be several butterflies in stomachs, and you and/or the Assistant Director of Ceremonies should be there as a totem for them to gather round and gain mutual support. Remind all participants to look to you if they need a prompt or guidance where to go next, and try to smile – it has a wonderfully calming and reassuring effect, because if you look tense and worried, it can be contagious.

The other people you should look out for are the Master and the Secretary. Both may have breaking news that additional items will be necessary – the Master may have picked up items of importance during his travels around other lodges since the last meeting, while the Secretary may have some recent correspondence from Grand or Provincial Grand Lodge that has to be acted upon. If there has been a very recent death in the lodge, or of a senior Officer in Grand Lodge or the Province, then the lodge may be asked to stand as a mark of respect for departed merit, a few words may be read in honour of his passing, and some Officers may be wearing black rosettes. Hopefully the grapevine has worked before the meeting, with the Master or Secretary having already warned you, but always expect the unexpected.

There may be some visitors wanting to see you. If you have any dignitaries attending, then they will probably make themselves known to you, so that you can inform them of the lodge's method of operating and they can check any other details that they need to know. You may also have some members introducing their guests and confirming that they can vouch to having sat with them in open lodge previously. They will certainly introduce any guests who are Entered Apprentices or Fellowcrafts, because they probably require one of the lodge aprons to wear. Also there may be some newcomers as guests who have not been before and do not know any member, and they should produce their Grand Lodge Certificates and letters of good standing from their own lodges, and then they need proving. This you may do, or delegate it to your Assistant Director of Ceremonies or the Junior Warden, and you may want to remind them that the visitor only needs to be proved in the highest degree that the lodge will be going into during the meeting. The Assistant Director of Ceremonies or Junior Warden should report back to you that all is well, as you are on behalf of the Master the ultimate guardian that all Masonic protocol has been followed on a lodge night.

With regard to seating, it is usual for the Grand Officers and often the Provincial Grand Officers to be seated on the Master's right hand (to the north east), and lodge Past Masters to be seated on his left hand (to the South East). You also have to allow for lodge Officers to be seated appropriately, with the Immediate Past Master next to the Master on his left hand side, and the Chaplain next to him, and possibly then you and the Assistant Director of Ceremonies. Some lodges prefer the Director of Ceremonies to be at the immediate right hand of the Master, so that he has two sources of guidance next to him throughout the meeting. If another Past Master is to occupy the Chair for a while in the meeting, then allow an extra place for the Master to be seated, and if there is a Past Masters' night then allow a few extra seats for the lodge Officers to be seated.

Opening Business of the Lodge

Your first duty may be to form an incoming procession for the Master, and this may include not only his Officers but also the lodge and visiting Past Masters and Masters of other lodges. An example of the processional order into and out from the lodge room is given in the Appendix. Newcomers may need a quick word on the format, which can be perhaps to follow the Deacons, and stop when they stop and turn inwards to form a guard of honour for the Master as he makes his way to the pedestal. Then if the visitors peel away from the procession while the Wardens are placed in position, advise the visiting brethren where they should sit – perhaps Provincial Officers in the North East and Masters in the South East, etc., as your lodge tradition requires.

You then hope the previous nights of practice stand all of the Officers in good stead, as they go through the formalities of opening. If it starts well, it usually continues in the same vein; if it starts otherwise, then hope that at some time one Officer manages to speak correctly and confidently, and that the confidence spreads. Nod encouragement to the Deacons if they look to see when they should be opening the lodge furniture such as the tracing board, and also to the Immediate Past Master if he opens the Bible. Then enjoy the opening ode if you sing one and have not done so earlier, and sit down; some lodges follow the Master in sitting, while in others either the Master or you invites everyone to be seated.

Now you can let the Master go through the agenda items in turn. The Secretary may read the summons convening the meeting, a member may read an ancient charge, and then the minutes of the previous meeting may be read and put to the vote, either directly by the Master or after a formal proposition and seconding by two members, perhaps the Wardens. The Deacons or Secretary will carry the Minute Book for signing by the Master and possibly by the Wardens. The Secretary or Assistant Secretary may then summarise or read the minutes of the previous Lodge Committee meeting. The Treasurer may need permission to pay some accounts, and this may again need a formal proposition and seconding for acceptance, as required by the lodge bylaws. But all of these items are routine, and you will have run through them at several practices before, especially with a new Master and Officers after their installation and investiture, so there should be no surprises here.

You as Director of Ceremonies may have to enquire about the numbers staying to dine, if the meal is pre-booked or otherwise as there may be extras, and you will probably ask who is not staying for the festive board after checking that everyone has signed the attendance register. You or the Inner Guard may then inform the Tyler to tell the caterer that meals are required for the number in the Tyler's book, minus those who cannot stay, plus those who did not sign in, plus the initiate if there is one, as he will not have signed the book. A little mental agility will be required of you, but hopefully it is not too onerous.

Visitors, Processions and Salutes
Most visitors in the lodge room when the meeting began will have been briefed by their hosts as to the protocol in the lodge. However, some visitors may have arrived before their hosts, and do not seem to be totally *au fait* with the Hall layout and the organisation of the lodge. They may introduce themselves to you or the Secretary, but it would be useful if the lodge team looking after visitors – the Junior Warden and his Stewards (remember the Installation Addresses?) – could be charged to keep a lookout for such newcomers and welcome them and introduce them to the Master, etc. If you have someone from another Constitution, then he may have brought a letter of introduction from his Grand Lodge and/or United Grand Lodge. He will still need to prove himself and to produce confirmation of good standing within his lodge, as well as his Grand Lodge Certificate. The Secretary may read out that letter as soon as the lodge is opened, and you will of course escort the visitor to be formally greeted and welcomed by the Master on behalf of the lodge. You may have some visitors or even members who turn up late, and after due announcement of their names via the Inner Guard and Junior Warden, perhaps you, the Assistant Director of Ceremonies or one of the Deacons will escort them into the lodge room to formally greet the Master and apologise for being late. They will then be escorted to a suitable seat in the lodge room, which may vary depending on their ranks, for example, Provincial Officers in the North East.

It may be that the late visitor is well known in the lodge, but if not you should perhaps enquire which member can vouch for him. Some lodges organise their meetings to conduct their essential opening business and then formally introduce visitors, and they often request the vouching member to stand and confirm so individually. If the visitor is not known or vouched for, then he will have to be proved – by you, the Assistant Director of Ceremonies or the Junior Warden. If the lodge has a Past Master who is acting as Tyler, I cannot see why he should not prove any latecomer appropriately – and if it is an installation, a Junior Warden who is a Master Mason cannot prove an Installed Master in any case. The Tyler can then report through the Inner Guard that there is a visiting latecomer and he has already been proved. However, the occurrence is fairly rare, and the Junior Warden when being invested is informed that he has a special responsibility for the examination of visitors, so often it is he who will leave the lodge and return with confirmation that the visitor may be admitted. This has been done to me on a few occasions when I have been late and a newcomer, and as a suggestion it might be a nice touch for whoever proves the visitor to personally accompany him into the lodge room to introduce him and confirm that he has been proved, and then let him greet the Master.

If there is a special visitor, perhaps representing the Provincial Grand Master at the installation meeting, it would be a courtesy for him to be met on his arrival at the Hall and introduced to the Master, Secretary and candidate or Master Elect as appropriate. It is also probable that he will merit a special entrance into the lodge after it has opened. Some Provinces insist that the lodge should have opened into the third degree for such a reception, but others allow an entrance in the first degree so that the visitor can see the opening ceremonies of the other degrees. If the visitor is very senior, he will be accompanied by the Provincial Director of Ceremonies or one of his Deputies, and you will leave everything to him. If, however, you need to organise the reception, you will probably leave the lodge room and then re-enter to announce the visitor and other senior guests in the accompanying procession. This is a time when the Secretary needs to have forewarned you who is coming, so that you have an idea of the list of titles you will have to reel off. If your memory is not as sharp as it used to be, there is no crime in having a crib sheet to read from – it is more important to make the correct pronouncements rather than a near miss. If the Deacons did not accompany you out of the lodge, you will request them to join you at the door of the lodge room, and you will lead the procession to the East. Probably the Deacons will follow you, spaced slightly apart, so that when they and the rest of the procession turn inwards, they will form a guard of honour for the principal visitor to walk through in order to greet the Master. You will probably introduce the dignitary to the Master, so that he can be formally welcomed by the head of the lodge.

Once the visitors are seated, you may conduct the salutations to those whom your lodge regularly salutes; some lodges perform these towards the end of the meeting, near to or in the risings, although as a form of welcome it seems a little late, but each lodge has its own traditions. Remember that salutes are silent, and greetings are noisy. All salutes begin with a step, as with all grips except the pass grip, while the sign of reverence has neither a step nor is it cut afterwards. One routine you may adopt is to stand, give the recipient of the salutes a court bow, request the brethren below that rank to stand, call upon them to give a number of salutes of the degree in which the lodge is opened, ask them to make a half-turn to the East and come to order, lead the salutes, request the brethren to be seated, another court bow to the recipient, and return to your seat.

Salutations are relatively straightforward if one remembers that they are received on the basis of the respective Provincial or Grand Rank held by the recipient. A list of Masonic ranks and the salutations to which they are entitled is given in the Appendix for easy reference.

In the unlikely event that the Grand Master, Pro Grand Master, Deputy or Assistant Grand Master are to attend the meeting, relax because the reception and salutation of the distinguished visitor will be handled by the Grand or a Deputy Grand Director of Ceremonies.

The salutations will normally begin with the Provincial (Metropolitan) Grand Master, his Deputy and Assistants (in the Metropolitan Grand Lodge this may include Metropolitan Grand Inspectors), and these will be saluted first, followed by the Grand Officers and then the Provincial Grand Officers. There is, however, a school of thought that says that only the senior officer present should be saluted and no other; custom and practice will dictate accordingly.

If it is the custom to salute Grand Officers then it will be necessary to check their respective ranks. Certain ranks are entitled to the appellation Right Worshipful and as such receive a salutation of seven, whilst others are entitled to the appellation Very Worshipful and as such receive a salutation of five. All other Grand Officers are entitled to receive a salutation of three.

After the Grand Officers have been saluted it may be considered appropriate to salute Provincial Grand Officers. It is usual to name and salute separately the representative of the Provincial Grand Master, or perhaps the senior Past Provincial Officer present, who will receive a salutation of three, unless entitled to a greater number as previously indicated.

It may be your lodge custom to name any other acting ranks that are visiting, and immediately after the new Provincial honours or promotions are conferred your lodge may like to formally congratulate those members who have been honoured in this way. The order of precedence for both Grand and Provincial Grand Officers is detailed in the Book of Constitutions.

Depending on circumstances it may be appropriate to share the workload with your Assistant Director of Ceremonies.

Before the closing business of the lodge, the dignitaries may express a desire to retire early from the lodge. This usefully deals with some of the bar traffic before the bulk of the attendees arrive after the meeting has closed, and the order will normally be the reverse of the equivalent incoming procession. One point to bear in mind, and the Provincial workshops will certainly have alluded to this, is that in many Provinces it is protocol for the representative or the most senior member of the Grand or Provincial Grand Officers to be conducted to his place at the head of the procession only after everyone else is in place. Some Provinces prefer you to take the hand of the Grand Officer for example and guide him into his place; others prefer you to lead in front of him, so check Provincial protocol. If the person being escorted is elderly, he may appreciate a hand to lean on, but you can have discussed this with him before the meeting began. The Deacons may cross their wands for the dignitaries to exit underneath, and when they have all gone, you and the Deacons return to your places, and everyone relaxes.

Other Items of Business
If there is to be no ceremony to be worked or demonstrated, it is probable that a lecture may be delivered, and you will obviously have been

introduced to the speaker. Each will have his own preferences for delivering his talk, some wanting to use a lectern if available, others wishing to move around the lodge room, perhaps pointing out various features during their presentation, or he may have brought his own visual aids. You will need someone to put the lectern in place if required (Assistant Directors of Ceremonies have their uses at times), and you yourself will accompany the speaker to the position from where he will begin his talk. If he is using electronic facilities, such as projectors or computer images, then the appropriate equipment will have been prepared ready for placing on the lodge room floor, but such special aids will probably have been set up by the speaker himself beforehand. After his talk and perhaps some questions, he will need escorting back to his seat, and possibly the Master, or you, or some other brother will have a short speech of thanks to deliver, but between you and the Secretary you should be aware of some of the content of the lecture, and such a speech can have been partly rehearsed at least in draft before the meeting. You should note that the content of some lectures requires the lodge to be called off and on again, and this is performed mainly by the Junior Warden – ensure that he and the Master are aware of these short extra pieces of ritual.

With candidates for initiation, joining members and the conferring of honorary membership, there is a ball ballot. The ballots can be taken all together, but if the allowed number of black or nay balls is exceeded, then the ballots need to be repeated as individual ones (you may deem it preferable to combine honorary and joining membership ballots, but leave candidates for initiation separate). The bylaws will indicate how many black balls are allowed whilst still not rejecting the candidate, and while Grand Lodge allows up to two black balls before there is an unsuccessful ballot, some lodges reduce that number to one or even none. The Deacons can either distribute a black and a white ball to each member (using the one-drawer ballot box; the two-drawer aye/nay box requires only one ball to be distributed), or remain at the Secretary's table to hand them out (whichever your lodge prefers). If it is the first time they have performed this task, they may be looking at you for confirmation that they are doing it correctly. The Deacons must give out the balls to members wishing to join in the ballot, otherwise by mistake or deliberately a member may take more than one ball and the ballot may be adversely affected. The ballot box must be shown to the Master prior to the ballot, to confirm there are no lingering balls from previous ballots, and you or the Deacons may do this. The members vote in turn, and the ballot box is taken to the Master, perhaps by you, to ascertain the outcome, which the Master declares, and the Wardens will confirm the result in turn if that is your lodge custom, but the ballot box drawer should not be displayed to everyone. Afterwards the unused balls are collected, and this needs to be secret as well, so the balls are returned into the same or another box or into a bag.

In the annual business meeting, or the meeting preceding the installation, there will be the ballots for the Master Elect, the Treasurer, and the Tyler if required (if the last-named is a member of the lodge, he can be appointed with the other Officers). Because of the range of members who are eligible for the offices, and the Master Elect for example can be a time-served Warden, a Past Master of yours or any other lodge, or even the Master of another lodge (by dispensation), paper ballots are used for the Master Elect and Treasurer. The Deacons will normally hand out the slips for the ballots, and you may allow them to remove their gloves if this makes the handling of the paper more efficient. They collect the completed slips for the Master to scrutinise, perhaps reading out loud the names on the first returns, although strictly only the result needs to be announced, and the lucky winner normally stands to acknowledge his good fortune. The Tyler's election, if he is not appointed, only requires a show of hands, as is the case with the confirmation of the minutes and propositions regarding the lodge finances. In more recent times, when there is only one name put forward for each of these offices, then a declaration can be made rather than taking a physical ballot, but if this is the case the necessary details will have been included on the summons by the Secretary, as any member can on the night request that a ballot takes place.

Other people may be elected at the business or other meeting, such as auditors, Group and Masonic Hall representatives, and each will need to be formally proposed and seconded. Normally the Secretary earmarks several members to perform these actions, and the votes are by a show of hands. Each of the elected members may respond to thank the brethren for the new-found or continued confidence in their capabilities. It may be usual to then receive the Almoner's report, the Charity or Festival representative's report, and reports from other appointees as required.

Closing the Meeting

The Master then initiates the final part of the meeting by asking if there is any other business to be transacted within the lodge, and this may include propositions and notices of motion, the former perhaps referring to potential new lodge members, and the latter possibly to the Treasurer wanting to raise the subscriptions again. The Master then enquires if there is any correspondence from Grand Lodge, Provincial Grand Lodge, or from anyone else, a sequence which is informally known in many lodges as 'the risings', because he and perhaps the Wardens may rise in turn to announce each enquiry.

The Secretary will summarise each set of correspondence, and after the first two the Grand Officers and the Provincial Grand Officers may respectively bring greetings and perhaps congratulations on how the meeting has gone. They may also choose to retire early, and you will organise the formal processions as discussed before. On the third rising all visitors may bring greetings, or you may – at an installation for example – limit the reply to one. It is a shame if you do impose a limit, because each visitor is an ambassador of his lodge and may be from a different Province or Constitution, and a few words from each lodge represented takes only a little extra time. If you encourage a spokesman for each visiting lodge to respond briefly, and you can emphasise the brevity, then it may be better that you walk around the lodge room in a clockwise direction to stand opposite each brother speaking, so all are confident that by catching your eye their turn will come.

The Senior Warden may then request the lodge members to stand and bring their own greetings to their Master, who after thanking all of the speakers will gavel to begin closing the lodge. The interchanges are shorter than in the opening, and after the Immediate Past Master has closed the Bible and returned to his place, you will begin forming the retiring procession, perhaps while the closing hymn is being sung. This may be done by you or the Assistant Director of Ceremonies walking round the lodge and picking up the Tyler, Inner Guard, Deacons and Wardens in turn, or you may have rehearsed it so that they form the procession on their own.

You will then bring in the Master and any dignitaries left behind, perhaps a Grand Officer in your own lodge, and acting Provincial Officers not requested to be in the guard of honour for the previous retiring processions. In some lodges, if Past Provincial ranks are also invited, then the lodge room would be almost empty, which is not particularly desirable. Your lodge may also invite the Masters of other lodges to join the final procession, and it is a courtesy that is always well received; they are after all the titular heads of their lodges, and it should always be a pleasure to receive them into your lodge as visitors. You then request the procession to leave, followed by other visitors, possibly in order of seniority if you wish, and then lodge members. And your lodge room work is over; only the meal to cope with now.

Special Meetings
There are many special meetings that lodges can enjoy, including the consecration of a new lodge. They can also include banner dedications, the personal celebrations of members such as the 50th or 60th anniversary of their initiation. Similarly, the lodge will have anniversaries to celebrate such jubilees, centenaries, sesquicentenaries, bicentenaries and even in rare instances 250th anniversary celebrations. For the lodge Director of Ceremonies these will be a joy, because the proceedings will be handled either by the Province, or Grand Lodge. Whilst you may be asked to assist, the burden of responsibility will be shifted from your shoulders, so you can enjoy the meeting along with the rest of your members.

The Craft Ceremonies

Preparation

Of course, the above section has skirted round the main events of most lodge meetings, the ceremonies in the three degrees. This is where the lodge team of Officers combine to reproduce their perfect ceremony as at the prior practice meeting and, if they do so, you can relax. If it does not go perfectly, there may be plenty for you to do. It is not perhaps surprising that when a ceremony starts off being less than perfect, it can go steadily downhill thereafter. You need to be vigilant, to check if any Officer is glancing at you for last-minute corrective advice where he is going or for a prompt, and your brain will be going through every word and action in the ceremony in order to assist instantly if called upon. This is no easy task, as most Directors of Ceremonies will testify, and you should share the load where possible with your Assistant Director of Ceremonies, perhaps splitting up sections of the ceremony, or one following the Assistant Officers and especially the Deacons, and the other looking after the Principal Officers. Make sure that your back-up prompter is not falling asleep during the ceremony, which may start very well and lull everyone into a false sense of security, only for a prompt to be required and not to be instantly forthcoming.

The Officers should be confident about where the action is to take place and the sequence of events, as hopefully all will have attended the prior practice. If any have missed that meeting, then you should have a quick word with them immediately before the lodge meeting, or even previously by telephone after they missed the practice, so that they are able to perform to their best abilities. If they go slightly wrong, then hopefully a few hand signals or quiet words of advice will correct events before they go too far from the desired format.

But in the case of an initiation, your work should have started some time before the ceremony. The candidate is someone who has not been to a Masonic meeting before. Even if he has attended social functions in the meeting place before, he will have realised that the business of the night is much more formal, and will possibly have seen various brethren walking round in their regalia. It would be a nice touch if you requested the proposer and/or seconder to bring the candidate to you so that you can introduce yourself to him and help to put his mind at ease on the subject of what is to befall him during the evening. You can in very general terms outline some aspects of the ceremony, such as for him to repeat what the Deacon tells him, and follow his instructions with regard to moving within the lodge. He will be interacting with several Officers during the meeting, and being blindfolded, he will have to rely on what he hears. There is no harm in introducing him to the Inner Guard, Deacons, Wardens and Master, so that he can listen to their voices and will be able to recognise them during the ceremony, even if he is not sure where he is in the room during the first part of the ceremony. And after all, you are welcoming a new member into the lodge, and possibly one who has interacted socially with the lodge for several months, so do your best to welcome him into his new Masonic family accordingly.

The Three Degree Ceremonies
So without going into minute detail over every ceremony, much of which has been covered in the books for the Assistant and Principal Officers, what are the key details in each? In the second and third degrees, the candidate has his test questions to answer, and the Deacon should be able to help him answer if he needs assistance. If you have two candidates, then you or the Immediate Past Master may act as an additional 'Master' for the entrusting, rather than the Master repeating that part for the second candidate. After he or they have retired, the lodge is opened in the higher degree, and any floor preparations made, possibly by the Deacons; ensure that they lay out the various items as you want, and no-one minds a few whispered instructions at this stage, or even the Deacons approaching you for additional instructions. You may note that there is no need to hide the lower degree tracing boards when opening into the second and third respectively; as the Master normally states when closing down, work is resumed – not restarted - in the lower degrees.

Before the candidate enters, check that you hear the appropriate password from him while being questioned by the Inner Guard. When he steps into the room, quickly check that the Tyler has prepared him properly, and if not you may have to go across to make the necessary adjustments – and you will have to do so rapidly in the third because of the reduced visibility away from the door. The circuits of the lodge should be accomplished without any problem, but watch in case the Deacon fails to halt before the final circuit. Then the candidate will approach the East in due form and with the appropriate number of steps and, unless this enactment is completely haywire, leave it uncorrected – to make the candidate repeat it properly will be lost on him, as he does not yet know there is a different method; the visitors will put whatever they have seen down to the idiosyncrasies of your lodge, and you can kill the Deacon later!

The Master should cope with the obligation and the short sections before and after, with the Immediate Past Master or you or the back-up prompter helping where needed. While the obligation is being taken, in many lodges the Deacons cross their wands over the kneeling candidate. In some lodges the Director of Ceremonies places his wand as an additional central support to their crossed wands, while in others the Director's wand is held horizontal between the Deacons' so as to make an equilateral triangle – you should join in as your lodge traditions decree. The Master or others will go through the next stages of the ceremonies – the signs and penalties in the first two, the circuit round the Wardens. If again you have two candidates, then you or the Assistant Director of Ceremonies may follow the candidates and Deacons around the lodge, to act as a second 'Warden' for the grip or token. Alternatively, you may have Past Masters strategically placed next to the Wardens' pedestals so that they can perform the same duty. Then follows the investiture of the new apron, and the moralisation on the working tools before the candidate leaves the room. Your main role will be waiting to assist with any prompts. There is a longer build-up in the third, with the Wardens taking over from the Deacons, and any oddities in how they do so are thankfully difficult to spot in the reduced lighting. You will have to rely on the three Principal Officers helping one another if needed – they are after all close to each other - and then the candidate receives his introduction to the penalties and signs before retiring.

All of the ceremonies follow on with additional explanations on what has been enacted so far, the third including the working tools in this latter section. You may have the explanations of the tracing boards and the charges included in this section, so there is not a great deal of movement around the lodge room, but there are a lot of words for you to follow should any brother require your assistance. On the other hand, in these sections it is often the more capable ritualists who are called into play, and hopefully you will have little to do.

The Installation Ceremony

The installation is different, because there are the open parts of the ceremony and the inner workings. Life becomes much more fun for you, because the Installing Wardens may be different from the regular lodge Officers, and your lodge may have a tradition of inviting Masters or senior brethren of other lodges to fill these positions. If the latter is the case, then hopefully they will have attended your installations before and will have an idea of what is expected of them, and they will obviously be invited to your practice meetings so that they can run through what they have to do. You may already think that it is difficult enough for your own lodge Officers to follow your lodge traditions, but now you will have to possibly persuade people inured in their own lodge traditions to temporarily adopt yours for one meeting. Hopefully they are willing volunteers, and so will put in the requisite work.

The installation meeting also involves the participation of many other lodge members, to present the Master Elect, to address the new Principal Officers the brethren and all of the Officers as required, and presenting the working tools in the various parts of the ceremony. Usefully they are all stand-alone pieces that can be learned in isolation by the respective people and, as long as they know where to deliver the items from, they may not necessarily want to go through the passages in a practice meeting. You might encourage all the juniors who are participating to demonstrate their capabilities in the practice meeting, because for them it will be a relatively new experience performing parts of the ritual in the lodge room and in front of probably many more attendees than at other meetings. Some lodges expect the new Master to address all of his Officers in full, so the Master Elect may well want to rehearse all of the addresses in front of an audience for his own peace of mind.

For the installation, as with most special lodge occasions, your members may be in dinner suits or formal morning attire, and all Provincial and Grand Officers may according to local custom wear full dress regalia. Because the installation is such a different ceremony, you cannot relax as you may have been able to do at previous lodge meetings. You and the Secretary will probably arrive earlier than normal to ensure everything is laid out properly, including reserved seats in the lodge room and place cards on the meal tables. You will also have a list of people performing different aspects of the ceremony, and you will want to check each of them as they arrive, otherwise you will rapidly need to identify some willing volunteers to fill in for them. You will certainly have a senior member of the Province coming as the representative of the Provincial Grand Master, and he may be attended by other Provincial Officers including the Provincial Grand Director of Ceremonies or one of his Deputies. With such an entourage, much of the processing and saluting duties are lifted off your shoulders, which is always welcome, although in the current times of smaller lodges these large attending escorts are possibly less in evidence than previously.

You will ensure that the Master realises that, if the Deputy or Assistant Provincial Grand Master is present, then not only can he demand entrance to the lodge, but he would also expect to receive the gavel of the lodge from the Master. This is done by the Master holding the head of the gavel in the left hand and resting the handle, pointing towards the dignitary, on the right wrist or forearm. In all likelihood the dignitary will receive it with courtesy and return it to the Master so that he can continue with the installation, although sometimes he will retain the gavel and occupy the Master's chair for a short time if he has a presentation of his own to make.

After the entrance of the dignitaries, it may be your lodge custom for the Officers to line up and hand in their collars of office to the Master, which not only lets him thank them personally, but he can pass the collars to you or the Assistant Director of Ceremonies or Immediate Past Master to place on a hanger ready for investing the new Officers. I never cease to be surprised how few lodges that request their Officers to line up in this manner, juniors first or last, manage to muddle through the seniority issue, which is probably stated every month on their summons as a reminder. However, an alert Immediate Past Master can make adjustments in the order as the collars are being handed to him so that they are ready for distribution to the new Officers, or perhaps during the pause before inviting juniors back into the lodge room you can rearrange them. Keep a note of any lodge Officers who cannot attend the installation meeting, as they will not be lining up to hand in their collars. You will need to ensure that their collars are in the lodge room and inserted at the appropriate place, as they may be transferred to other lodge members who are present at the meeting.

You may then need to escort all of the Installing Officers to their respective places in the lodge room. The Master Elect is presented, possibly by you or another senior member of the lodge, and obligated in the second degree, and most of the work is done by the Master – and also the Master Elect if he has been asked to learn his first obligation. The lodge then opens in the third degree, and the remaining juniors leave the lodge room. There may be an entrusting if your lodge uses extended inner working, then the Board of Installed Masters is opened and the inner working conducted, led by the Installing Master, but possibly assisted by other Installed Masters.

The juniors then return sequentially in the three degrees, and you or the Installing Master ask them to salute the new Master in passing, and then to greet him with three or five salutes as appropriate. It is very useful to rehearse this with the juniors at the practice meetings, and perhaps if they do not always attend the practices you can go through the sequence after the previous lodge meeting, or even arrange to meet them early before the installation starts. It does not look professional to have to tutor them in the actual ceremony, and yet many lodges seem to do so – which might imply there is no confidence that the juniors have been properly educated? You will restrict the incomers to Master Masons, Fellowcrafts and Entered Apprentices in the separate degrees, or split what may be a large number of Master Masons more evenly into three sets of juniors re-entering the lodge. You may also hand the working tools of each degree to those presenting them to the Master and, if these are juniors, a reassuring smile or wink may not go amiss in calming their nerves. And after the Master has closed down the lodge to the second and then the first degree, either you or the Immediate Past Master will adjust the tracing boards and the square and compasses. After the Entered Apprentice's tools have been explained to the new Master, he will be presented with the Book of Constitutions and the lodge bylaws, unless these are included in the address to the Master (which from its text actually appears to be a more appropriate time for the presentation). If your lodge has a Hall Stone Jewel, the collarette will then be passed on from the Immediate Past Master to the new Master.

The Master then appoints and invests his Officers for the year. As Director of Ceremonies you may immediately begin your escorting duties, or you may leave the first few to the Installing Master until you are appointed. Whoever is orchestrating events, he will have to remember that Past Masters are presented to the Master's left hand side (where the lodge Past Masters are seated), and juniors to his right hand side. If you and/or the Assistant Director of Ceremonies are on escort duty, remember to be not carrying your wand until you have been formally presented with it at your investiture, and indeed you may decide not to carry it throughout this part of the ceremony. When you are on escort duty, you and the Assistant Director of Ceremonies should be able to co-operate efficiently to collect the various members and their emblems of office, present the new Officers to be invested to the Master, and then escort them to their places around the lodge room. You may agree that you will collect the people, and the Assistant Director of Ceremonies the objects, or you may take it in turns to look after each Officer to and from the Master.

If you have an honorary organist, he cannot wear that collar of office, but it would be a nice touch after the Tyler's investiture for the Master to formally thank him for past and future services, perhaps by you escorting him to and from the East. Then follows the addresses to the Master, Wardens and brethren, and each person delivering an address may require escorting to and from a suitable place in the lodge room. Some lodges invite the representative to take part in the ceremony, and will often suggest that he might deliver the address to the brethren, so that particular escorting duty needs to done formally. Hopefully you know this address well because, standing close behind him, you will be in the perfect position to prompt the representative quietly if and when required.

After the investiture of a Past Master's jewel to the Immediate Past Master and perhaps a congratulatory speech from the representative, the lodge reverts to its normal business mode, which has already been covered previously so, apart from the probable early retirement of the representative and dignitaries, you should see a familiar sequence of events to ordinary lodge meetings. If there is a cheque to give to the representative, it would probably be most neatly fitted into the few words that the Master says in answer to the representative's comments. After the close of the meeting, there is the banquet to oversee, which makes the installation meeting a marathon for any Director of Ceremonies.

If the Master Elect is unable to attend on the normal installation date, the lodge will try to obtain a dispensation to move to a date when he can be there. If he still cannot attend, and there is no time to ballot for another Master Elect, then the current Master must continue in office for a second year, or even a third year by dispensation (BoC 107, 108). In these circumstances the Master may simply be proclaimed as he is to continue in office and saluted accordingly. He will then invest the new lodge Officers. If, however, the Master is going to stay on for a second year, and he cannot as Master Elect attend the installation, then it can be proclaimed that he is continuing in office for the ensuing year, and another Installed Master will invest the new lodge Officers in his stead. This will be a very short installation meeting, because the proclamation can be in the first degree, so there are no obligations, no second or third degree opening and closing or tools (no-one to present them to). If these circumstances have never previously arisen in your lodge, you may request the Secretary to seek guidance from the Provincial Office on the preferred format for the meeting.

Out of Lodge Functions

Installation and General Lodge Meals

At festive boards, meals and social functions, you as Director of Ceremonies are kept busy for the whole time, as organiser and toastmaster. An example of a seating plan at meals after lodge meetings is given in the Appendix. Some lodges first request the presence of the Master in the Provincial assembly room, so those Officers can formally toast his good health for the coming year, and you will have to see that he excuses himself from other people to be there punctually. At an installation or a major meeting, the representative may also request to meet the brethren of the lodge less formally, and you will accompany him in order to introduce the different members to him, both the juniors and the seniors. In bygone days many representatives and senior Provincial Officers were very aloof and tended to mix only with their peers; these days there is a greater intermixing of Masonic status, and the Craft is the better for it.

You may start the formal proceedings by announcing that the Master is about to enter the dining room, perhaps with the senior distinguished guests, and you then lead him to his seat at the top table. The usual form is that, if the Provincial Grand Master is present, the announcement would be to "Receive the Master, Worshipful Brother.... accompanying the Provincial Grand Master, Right Worshipful Brother... and accompanied by ....". If it is another distinguished brother attending, then the announcement would be to "Receive the Master, Worshipful Brother.... accompanied by ....".

It is a courtesy if those brethren whom you pass on the way to the top table do not have their backs to the Master, and depending on the geography of the dining room they may stand back from their chairs to let him pass between, or turn outwards as he passes them. You then call silence for the Chaplain to pronounce grace and afterwards ensure the Master is seated – the rest should follow his example, but if not then invite them to do so.

There may be wine-taking at the meals, especially the installation banquet, and a selection of toasts is given in the Appendix, although your lodge may have other wine-taking traditions that they enjoy. Some lodges will take wine after every course of the meal, while others will have them all after the first or possibly extending to after the second course, in order to let the remainder of the meal be eaten in peace. You will announce each wine-taking after the Principal Officers have gavelled for attention, and draw the Master's chair back slightly to help him stand. It is usual for the representative to take wine with not only the Master, but also with the rest of the brethren, and you will offer him the same courtesy. You and the Treasurer will need to keep an eye on the wines on the tables if it is provided by the lodge, to ensure the Stewards keep an ample but not necessarily profuse supply for the brethren and particularly the guests to enjoy.

After the meal is over, and possibly the caterers have cleared away the plates, you will call on the Chaplain to return thanks, and then you start on the formal toast list, possibly after singing a verse of the National Anthem if you have not done so in lodge. Each Province will have a preferred list of toasts to be taken, and you and the Master simply follow this, an example of which is given in the Appendix. It will be helpful if you run through the pronunciation of the toast list before the installation day, to ensure the Master and Wardens manage to avoid the "Programme Master" and the "Provisional Grand Master" etc., as any mistakes they may make are evidence of a lack of tuition from you. Sometimes the Master proposes all of the toasts before his own, while in other lodges the Wardens assist, perhaps one proposing toast 3 and the other toast 5, and you will take the toast list to them and call on each in turn to propose them. The neatest way is for the Master to gavel when you are behind the person who is to propose the toast; you then call the brethren to attend to the next toast, and the proposer explains to whom the toast is directed. It is better to avoid numbering the toast in your announcement, and it usefully means you do not have to keep a running total of the toasts already taken. Some lodges have traditional ways of responding to toasts – by applause, by one knock, or perhaps by firing. If the last, then the Master or you will need to lead the brethren, so be sure you remember how it is done.

There may be a reply to toasts 3 and 5 by a Grand Officer and a Provincial Grand Officer respectively, or they may both be answered in one reply to toast 5. If the respondent is the representative, or even when a very distinguished guest is present at a meeting other than the installation, some Provinces request a short biography of that person is given by the Master or Director of Ceremonies. In this situation these people will fortunately have prepared such a *résumé*, and you merely read it all or just some highlights by agreement with them. You then help them to their feet (not insinuating that they are by this time incapable of standing unaided) by easing out the chair as they rise, and hope they find something nice to say about the lodge and its workings. And you can be assured that they will have seen almost everything, and that they will report back to Province on the state of the lodge if they have been requested to do so. You should remain standing behind the person, ready to assist him in reseating himself by easing in the chair again, and do not start pushing the chair prematurely against his knees as a sign he should perhaps consider finishing his speech, whatever you think of it.

If at the installation meeting the lodge defers the charity collection until the banquet, you may arrange for it to follow the toast to Provincial Officers. You will need to have organised the Charity Steward and Stewards to collect the alms as quickly as possible, and the Treasurer to count it so the total can be announced later in the evening if your lodge does so. The next toast is to the Master and may be given by the Immediate Past Master or another brother – perhaps his proposer into Masonry, and you will need to introduce him, having warned the Master to keep an eye on you and gavel as soon as you have arrived behind the chair of that person. After he has finished, if it is an installation, there may be the Master's song delivered by members or visitors, and they probably will not need any introduction, as the accompanist will provide his own. Note that in some lodges they did not allow smoking before this song out of consideration for the vocal chords of the singer(s), but nowadays most if not all lodges do not allow smoking at all. If your lodge and meeting place do permit smoking, then appropriate permission will be given, usually not before the second toast of the evening.

It is not unusual for a first-time Master to become emotional on hearing the Master's song sung, perhaps by a long-standing friend or even a family member and, if the lodge allows people to leave their seats for a short time after the song to greet their friends individually, this will allow him time to recover. If everyone stays seated, you may pause for a short while before inviting him to respond for the same reason. After his speech he may finish by toasting the Installing Master and his team, or make a separate speech, and the Immediate Past Master may or may not respond. If the representative has to leave early, he will normally wait until after the Master's speech, and you may lead him out of the room but obviously you cannot go with him to see him off the premises, so it is a good idea to delegate one or more of the senior lodge members to accompany him as a courtesy, and they can afterwards rejoin you in the dining room if they wish to do so.

There then may follow the toast to Masonic charities, and if the total collected earlier is known, the Charity Steward or whoever proposes the toast can inform the assembly of the sum raised; otherwise the Master can do so in his closing remarks. The toast to absent brethren may come next, or if your tradition is to keep to a specific time it may have already been taken and, if there is a sung verse or two, you will need to check that the pianist is ready to accompany the singing. After this there may be a toast to the Founders at installations, and whoever has been assigned this task – some lodges ask juniors to do this - you will need to locate him and introduce him accordingly.

You have now arrived at the toast to the visitors, and this is probably to be proposed by the Junior Warden or ostensible steward of the lodge, although some lodges allow others to do it on occasions. If it is traditional that the toast is preceded by a listing of the lodges represented by the visitors to be read out or summarised, then ensure that the Tyler's book or attendance sheet is with the person proposing the toast. You may remind the proposer that he should couple the name and lodge affiliation of the respondent before the glasses are raised, and you then make your way to the person so named. This hopefully should not be the first time he has been informed that he is expected to reply, a service normally performed by you or the Secretary immediately after the lodge meeting, unless beforehand the Master has already invited someone to do it. There may be more than one response, especially at installations and other major occasions, and you will call for order before each one speaks. You or the Master (by gavelling) will call on the Tyler for his toast, to be given either from near to where he was sitting or perhaps from behind the Master, and then you may call on the Master for the few final words. NOW you can heave a sigh of relief and begin to enjoy yourself, because your duties for the evening are at last over.

Social Events and Ladies' Functions

Your lodge may hold special meals for the brethren, such as Olde English Nights and other occasions where the emphasis is on enjoyment of the entertainment and possibly raising money for charity, and the toast list may be adapted. There may be very short or even no responses to the toasts, but all of the first five should be honoured. Hopefully a band of lodge members will have sorted out the bulk of the activities for the evening, and you effectively hand over to them, probably returning to introduce the toast to the visitors and the Tyler's toast at the end of the festivities.

Those lodges which after a meeting dine with their ladies occasionally or frequently will already be aware that the toast list is very truncated compared with occasions when only brethren are present, and the same applies to lodge socials and Ladies' Evenings. As Director of Ceremonies you primarily still attend on the Master and his lady at the first two types of events, but at the Ladies' Evening your primary responsibility is to look after the lady on her night. She will be making the response to the one toast of the night that requires it, and you should endeavour to assist in making what might be a nerve-racking time for her as comfortable as possible.

The Master and his lady may have greeted everyone on arrival in the function room, perhaps with formal introductions by you, and sometimes a photographer will take pictures to record the couples or groups. With modern technology the pictures can be on show after the meal if people wish to keep a souvenir of the evening. Once you have formally escorted the guests of honour to their places at the head of the top table and the meal has started, the Master and his lady will take wine with a series of guests, inserting some of their own requests in addition to the standard lodge wine-taking list.

When the meal is completed there may be presents to distribute to the ladies, and you will have organised table stewards to collect and give out the presents on their table. There may be table prizes, such as the flower decorations on the tables, and these may be drawn from ladies seated at each table after the name cards have been collected by the lodge Stewards, or possibly the Secretary has arranged duplicates to be available and obviate the need for such a collection – some people wish to keep such mementoes. The Junior Warden or another member will then be called on by you to propose the toast to the ladies, which will hopefully mention the support given to the Master by his lady in his year of office. The proposer may already have indicated to the Master the content of his speech, in case his lady wishes to include some comments about the proposition of the toast, and would appreciate the time to think through her response. The proposer may also present to the lady any gift that the lodge has collected for as a more enduring mark of appreciation for her work during the year, together with perhaps a bouquet of flowers if this has not been presented to her earlier.

The brother or brethren singing the ladies' song should require no introduction before they perform, although you may feel the need to call for silence before they begin; there should be no need, as the first few chords on the piano will quieten people down. You announce the Master's lady is eager to reply, and whether or not this is quite the case, she will stand to deliver her speech; and you remain behind her ready to ease her chair forward when she sits down again. During her speech she may wish to present some personal gifts of her own, perhaps to the Social Secretary and his lady, who will have been working very hard on their own or with a small committee to ensure that all aspects of a large function have been planned down to the last detail. You will have those gifts and perhaps bouquets of flowers ready to pass to the Master's lady at the appropriate times, and possibly also table prizes to give out if your lodge includes those as well and usually hands them over from the top table.

You can then escort the Master and his lady out of the function room at the end of the meal, perhaps after you have informed the guests if they need to vacate the room for a short time while it is rearranged for dancing and less formal seating. You may escort the principal couple onto the dance floor for them to start the first dance. The rest of the evening should continue without any intervention by you, unless the Master and his lady wish to say a few final words at the end of the evening, when you may need to form a circle of guests around the Master, his lady and probably their family to hear those closing comments. All in all, a long but hopefully satisfying evening for all of the ladies of the lodge, and especially for the principal lady on her night.

Lodge Amalgamations and Similar

It might seem odd, after dealing with the lodge ceremonial and social functions in some detail, to now bring up the topic of amalgamations. Perhaps twenty or so years ago there would have been no need for this section, but nowadays almost every Province and Group, especially in the larger Provinces, has seen several lodge amalgamations. Sometimes these involve only two lodges, and sometimes more. There might even be lodges which decide to hand their warrants in and formally close them, and then several members from one lodge will become joining members of your lodge.

Now as Director of Ceremonies you have several sets of people within the lodge who have been brought up and become inured with different rituals. Your job is to create a cohesive whole from the several parts. If the joining lodges or members are happy with the host lodge's ritual, then there are no complications. But the new lodges may be assimilated better if some aspects of their own ritual continue to be practised in the new lodge, so that they can feel more at home in their new surroundings.

This does not mean that their version of one of the ceremonies is performed every time. You might suggest that, as a trial, the new members combine – as in a Juniors' or Past Masters' Night – to present one of their ceremonies. This will lay a gentle challenge at the feet of the new members, for them to show to the rest of the members why they think their ritual is so good. If the number of people joining is not enough to perform the whole ceremony, then add in some of the host lodge's members to make up the full cast. Then the whole lodge can discuss afterwards what they thought of it – is it better than what was formerly done? Are there some parts that were better? Or is it something to be performed occasionally as a change of scene?

And within these suggestions is another aspect to consider – allowing people other than the usual ritualists to perform parts from another ritual, especially if they have said that they enjoyed the new piece. Perhaps when they learn the parts for themselves, they can confirm in their own minds that the new ritual is an improvement on what was previously done. If the lot falls to some juniors on a Juniors' Night, then they may never have seriously learned anything else, so the new version is the first that they try to commit to memory. And whatever ritual is used, if it is presented well, then it will sound professional and may ensure that other people consider it further.

After several sessions with several people of the different lodges agreeing to take on ritual other than their own, all of the lodge members will be coming to an individual and joint consensus on what combination of rituals seems to be the best agglomeration, and perhaps the host lodge's ritual will be bent slightly to accommodate what will probably be quite small variations. If they are indeed small, and of the order of personal deviations that you as Director of Ceremonies will not interrupt in order to correct the person delivering the piece of ritual, then they probably lie within the noise of tolerance that all members will accept from their colleagues when they are participating in a ceremony. You have then derived a lodge ritual which encompasses the wishes of the lodge members and possibly includes some of the key items that the members of each of the previously solo lodges feel are particularly important to retain. After a few more years, you may decide to print a new copy of the lodge ritual, so that members are not leafing through old books with lots of footnotes about the changes that have been included.

Of course, the joining members may have some pieces of ritual that could be stand-alone additions to the single lodge ritual. There might be no harm in letting the piece be performed, in order to properly judge its merit. One example may be a short ceremony to welcome joining members. This is a more frequent occurrence than in bygone years, with lodge amalgamations and closures being quite widespread, so to have a short formal ceremony for them to be introduced to the lodge might be appropriate nowadays. It usually involves the Principal Officers (mainly the Master), with you as Director of Ceremonies escorting the newcomers after they have successfully come through the ballot. The new member is first addressed in the West, brought to the Master in the East to receive the lodge bylaws, etc., taken to each of the Wardens in turn, and then addressed again in the West before being escorted to a seat in the lodge.

Another piece of ritual may be the valedictory address. Some lodges perform this just before or after the lodge has been closed by the Senior Warden, as a reminder to the assembled brethren that before they quit the lodge room they should remember the lessons taught within the precincts of the lodge, and continue to emulate them when they re-enter the world outside. This may not necessarily be performed at every meeting, but perhaps reserved for the major lodge celebrations such as the installation and the Olde English Night, or possibly after each initiation and/or raising as well.

There will probably be far less resistance to the incorporation of a stand-alone piece than trying to modify the text of the existing ritual, as people are able to settle into a well-worn groove and almost coast along on auto-pilot. To start to change the sequence of items and the remembered internal prompts within the text will cause confusion in the minds of many lodge members, and they may be quite dogmatic in their objections to these introductions, whereas with a new stand-alone piece – especially involving you as Director of Ceremonies rather than themselves, they will more than probably go along with the trial. And lodges that have tried it normally seem happy to continue with it, and hence their ritual develops.

A further aspect of lodge amalgamations is that the lodge now has additional celebrations to plan for. Previously there was the installation night and perhaps an Olde English Night as the major lodge events of the year. The installation is also marking the anniversary of the creation of the lodge, and very often the date in the year will be close to the starting date of the lodge. With another lodge joining you, you can celebrate its anniversary as well – not by a second installation meeting, but perhaps by introducing another special event, and possibly with members of that second lodge putting on the Masonic part of the evening's entertainment, and perhaps even the social entertainment as well. If more than two lodges amalgamate together, then there will be more than one additional anniversary to build into the combined lodge calendar. The incorporation of several celebrations in the Masonic year will ensure that there are good attendances at all of them, as several members will probably invite the guests that they brought along to their own installations, and perhaps the new lodge will take on a more vibrant atmosphere than had been possible in the single lodge.

The Assistant Director of Ceremonies

It is unusual for someone to jump straight into the post of Director of Ceremonies; more normally he has understudied as his Assistant for a while. So if you aspire to be in charge of the lodge ceremonies, how do you go about it?

Knowing the Ritual

If you are going to perform as either the Director or his Assistant, you are going to have to know the lodge ritual comprehensively. There are some who assert that it is sufficient to know the choreography of the ceremonies, to orchestrate the incoming and outgoing processions, to escort people around the lodge, and to be able to give greetings to dignitaries. However, most lodges will be happier with someone who has a wide knowledge of the three degree ceremonies and the installation.

This does not necessarily mean that you have to know every word by heart, but you should be *au fait* with the most important sections of the ceremonies. These will certainly include the obligations and the addresses to the candidates or Officers, the working tools, and the first degree charge. These are the star items on any night, and to have a long, pregnant pause in the middle of one of these will spoil the whole presentation. So even if you agree that the Secretary or his Assistant, for example, will perform all of the prompting duties, it would be very useful for the lodge to know that you can confidently step in to assist at these points. And it has been said before, a wrong prompt can cause unwelcome and unnecessary confusion in the presenter's mind, so you do need to be confident that you are giving the correct prompt.

I do not think that many people will aspire to be the Director of Ceremonies if they are not good all-round ritualists. And this learning takes place almost at the start of any Masonic career. You learn the answers to the questions at the start of the second and third degree ceremonies, and at the same time you take in the questions so that each triggers the correct answer. You may then be invited to deliver the explanations of the working tools of the degrees, and possibly some of the other aspects of the ceremonies. If you are showing an aptitude for the ritual, then you may learn the explanations of the tracing boards, which will certainly demonstrate to lodge members that you have a capable memory.

Then as you go through the offices on the way to the Master's chair, you will be learning the choreography of the ceremonies as the Inner Guard and Deacon, and then as a Warden the interrogations of the candidates and the dialogues with the Master. Once installed as Master, you have the whole running of the lodge business and probably large chunks of additional ritual to deliver to the candidates, so you are progressively learning the whole of the ceremonies as you climb through the ranks. Even as Immediate Past Master you do not relax, because you are in the best position to help your successor if at any time he should need it – and this is just what he informs you that he wants when he collars you as Immediate Past Master.

In some ways, therefore, an appropriate time to become the Assistant Director of Ceremonies is the year after Immediate Past Master, while everything is fresh in your mind. This does not always happen, in which case you can volunteer for any part of the ceremony where a vacancy arises, either because the lodge always divides the ceremonies into several parts, or because someone cannot attend the lodge meeting as an Officer or otherwise. This keeps your mind actively going through the ceremonies being performed, and perhaps noticing aspects of the choreography that were not apparent to you before. This in turn means that the lodge members acknowledge your capabilities and enthusiasm, and the step into the office of Assistant Director of Ceremonies is seen as a natural one.

Once you have become the Assistant Director of Ceremonies, this is no time to relax with regard to lodge ritual. You should perhaps try to go through the ceremonies word for word, so that you can fill in any gaps in your knowledge, and also the choreography of when and how the different participants arrive at their appointed positions ready for the next parts of the ceremony. This is a useful exercise, because every Director wants to have reliable substitutes to have on hand if someone cannot turn up on the lodge night, so an Assistant who can turn his hand to almost anything at short notice is a very useful asset.

This is also the time when you might endeavour to learn some of the ancillary parts of the ceremonies – the explanations of the tracing boards, and charges in the second and third degrees, and other additional pieces of literature that your lodge includes in its ritual. These pieces may be quite lengthy, but as stand-alone items, if delivered with style, add another dimension to the ceremony and for the candidate. And it again demonstrates to the lodge that you are still growing in your Masonic knowledge and assimilating the lodge ritual even more deeply than hitherto.

Man Management

Now that you are in post as the Assistant, you have another perspective of the job to accommodate. Previously you could treat almost everything you did as a stand-alone job – you went to the right place in the lodge and delivered your part; you were in control of all of your actions. In this job, however, you see the reverse side of the coin – you are now assisting others to be in the right place, and they will have to deliver their parts on their own (or possibly with you just behind them if they need a prompt).

So you are now in the business of encouraging other people to perform well in the lodge, and these will include some who are not born ritualists. Fortunately most people want to perform well for their own satisfaction and also that of others, so they will follow useful advice with some eagerness. And your job is to ensure that they arrive in the right place via the correct route with the minimum of fuss, whether this is squaring the lodge, standing opposite the candidate to present something to him, or escorting him around the lodge room. If the other people participating in the ceremony can move quietly and confidently to where they need to go, then hopefully they will perform as well as they did at the more informal practice beforehand.

The characteristics of a Director of Ceremonies have been mentioned in some detail before, so will not be repeated here. But when dealing with other people, you will soon learn that everyone has their own way of assimilating information and then translating that into action. I am one of those who enjoys seeing several different ways of doing things, so that I can then select the method that suits me best. So one of the best ways to help someone to do something he currently has difficulty with, is to say "I have found that this works for me", and to show him how you would do it. Perhaps it is presenting a candidate to a Warden, so walk him through the choreography with him acting as candidate: wheel round to face the Warden, with him slightly in front of you, take a short step to come level with him, place the wand on the floor another 9 inches in front of you, so it can rest on your shoulder, make the sign, introduce the candidate, cut the sign, hold the wand, take the arm of the candidate so that he takes his step forward, makes the sign, etc. Then you become the candidate and he the Deacon, and let him go through it with you. You have thereby shown him a method of breaking down the item into single moves and which, when unhurried, will flow seamlessly from one to the other.

Once most people have become confident about the piece of choreography that concerns them, they are usually more than capable of delivering whatever part of the ceremony comes next. But as Assistant you have to know the choreography of every move in the ceremony, and the timing when people should start to move if, for example, more than one person needs to arrive at the same part of the lodge simultaneously. So you now have a roving eye, trying to take in everyone's movements in the lodge to ensure that all of the actions are fitting together as they should. Whilst in the actual ceremony it is the Director of Ceremonies who is in charge, you can in parallel be taking note of the items that could be tidied up next time they are done.

Duties of the Assistant Director of Ceremonies

These will cover all of those of the Director, although obviously they can be performed by only one person on the day. So it is probable that the lodge has normally seen the duties divided to some extent between the two of you. The Director will usually orchestrate the incoming and outgoing processions at the start and end of the meeting, with his Assistant either leading the processions or picking up the participants as he perambulates the lodge after the closing. It may well be that the salutations to any Grand Officers will be performed by one of you, and those to the Provincial Officers by the other. And if escort duties are required, to place people at different locations within the lodge room during ceremonies or to collect latecomers, then the Assistant may be asked to perform them.

It is likely therefore that the duties for a new Assistant will follow closely those of his predecessor, perhaps modified by the interpretation of the Director, who may also be new to the position. He may well discuss with you how to share the work, and it is useful to have such discussions before the installation. In that meeting both he and you are appointed and invested, and in many lodges the Director and his Assistant work together to ensure a smooth flow of lodge Officers are collected, presented to the new Master, and returned to their seats. Normally the Director will make the presentations, and the Assistant will collect and return the Officers, but there are lodges where they will take it in turns to perform the full escort and presentation duties for each individual. And there is nothing wrong with working together even before you are both appointed – collecting the Wardens, Chaplain, Treasurer and Secretary for example; it is just that you will not be carrying your wands until the Master has formally invested both of you with them.

Another area of lodge life where there may be a demarcation of duties will be in the lodge practices. If the Director cannot attend a practice, he will hope that his Assistant can do so. If there is more than one practice per month, then these may be designated junior and senior practices, the latter being a rehearsal for the lodge meeting ceremony, while the former may be for the juniors of the lodge to try out parts of the duties of the different Officers. In my first lodge the junior practice was in the hands of the Assistant, although the Director was often present in support. And to some extent this was a useful arrangement, as the younger Assistant was closer to the age of the juniors who were taking their first steps into the ritual of the lodge (we had several Stewards at the time), and could remember more clearly his own emotions trying those different offices that the incumbents seemed to have mastered with so little effort. So he could empathise better with the juniors. But the groundwork for future good ritualists in a lodge is laid in such practice meetings, and even those who were not very good at ritual at least became confident about the choreography of the ceremonies. In those days we had one meeting each year called a Junior Night, when the Stewards would take over the lodge offices up to Senior Deacon and take a candidate through a ceremony. It seemed a great honour at the time, and it did show the confidence of the older lodge members in our several abilities, and not one of the juniors so chosen let the lodge down on the night. Nor have any juniors that I have seen delivering parts of the ceremonies in other lodges, so if your lodge does not let their Masonic youngsters loose on the lodge floor, perhaps it is time to suggest that they do so.

As you become more confident in your role, the Director will feel happier if he is unwell or required elsewhere on a lodge night, as he will always want to leave the running of the lodge in capable hands. He may well ask a previous Director of Ceremonies, or a member who has had such experience from another of his lodges, to be your Assistant on the night, but only as a back-up to you rather than pulling all of the strings. This would be an opportunity for the lodge members to see that the lodge will be capably organised by you, so grasp it with both hands. Not that you should wish any illness on your Director, but if and when the time arises, you should be prepared. And good luck to you on the night.

Retirement

After a possibly long and hopefully enjoyable tour of duty as Director of Ceremonies, you can finally hand over to your successor. There is no fixed retirement date for the post, but some lodges like to change their Officers at least every five or so years because they want other members to try their hand at the different jobs, and it is recommended that if possible no tenure of office should exceed seven to ten years. Other lodges, once they have found a capable and willing volunteer and no others appear on the horizon, will allow him to continue as long as he wants, and he may eventually find it difficult to hand over if he has held the office for decades.

It is always useful to have a capable Assistant Director of Ceremonies working with you, especially when nearing your hand-over to a successor. Although some lodges make the Assistant Secretary a progressive office for juniors, very few will countenance a junior becoming an Assistant Director of Ceremonies, so this member is usually a successor in waiting. You may begin placing more of the workload on his shoulders leading up to the hand-over, and let him become accustomed to running affairs under your supervision. He will benefit if you can provide him with copies of the notes you have made for various occasions as the basis of his own checklists, and you will probably be explaining in greater detail the things that by now have become almost second nature to you.

As stated previously, you will probably have shared at least some of the workload with your Assistant Director of Ceremonies, perhaps letting him lead the salutations to Provincial Officers, escorting all latecomers or perhaps those who are not Grand or Provincial Grand Officers, placing and removing the kneeling stool, leading or organising the retiring procession at the end of the meeting. Some of the lodge practices, especially if your lodge has two before each meeting, you can delegate him to organise, perhaps putting the juniors through their paces less formally as they gain confidence. You may also have worked as a team at the installation meetings, with you collecting the people and him the items they will be presented with. In the year before hand-over, you may agree to delegate virtually all of the running of the lodge to him so that he has some practice runs at leading operations, and of course if you have missed a lodge meeting he will have taken over your role on that occasion.

Together you may also discuss who would be suitable to replace him as Assistant Director of Ceremonies when he steps up, because you both will have enjoyed working as an efficient team, and he will now require the same support as he gave to you.

Probably the most difficult job will be to sit and watch your successor in your shoes, so applaud him when he does well, and only volunteer advice when he asks – everyone has his own way of operating, and you will doubtless have brought your personality into the job when you started. So there may be slight differences, and some of the new ways may even prove to be better suited to the changing requirements of the lodge; all lodges have developed over the years as they have matured, and things that have historically resisted any change have usually ended up like the dinosaurs – extinct.

It is a demanding but very rewarding job, and hopefully you will be remembered among the best Directors of Ceremonies in the lodge. And as a last piece of advice for your successor, which probably stood you in good stead during your term of office:

"Remember that it's nice to be important,
but it's more important to be nice."

Appendix

What Each Officer of the Lodge Needs to Know from the Director of Ceremonies

Tyler

His place in any lodge procession;

How to inform the catering staff of dining numbers as soon as they are reported from the lodge room;

How to report the arrival of dignitaries or latecomers;

How to report the Junior Warden or Director of Ceremonies returning into the lodge room having left to prove the latecomer;

The preparation of the candidates for one degree is given in the ritual of the next degree ceremony, except the third which involves everything – use the book or printed lodge advice as an *aide-mémoire* if necessary;

Keep the candidate calm by talking to him, explaining the reasons for the preparation if possible;

The knocks on the lodge door may be Emulation or a specific lodge variation;

If not sure about the words of the Tyler from memory, use the book or prompt sheet when the candidate enters the lodge – it sets the scene for the whole ceremony, added to which the Inner Guard repeats almost exactly what the Tyler says, and any variation from the accepted words will make the Inner Guard question his own memory, and the problem may become contagious;

Ensure the re-dressing is as quick as possible – the rest of the lodge is in animated suspense until the candidate's return, although they may be receiving the Almoner's report and other items during the pause;

Ensure that the candidate has practised his salutes before his return, to give him added confidence in lodge;

When to enter and join in any retiring procession;

The Tyler's toast if required at the festive board, and where it should be delivered from (where he is sitting, at the end of the table, behind the Master, etc.).

Inner Guard

His place in any lodge processions;

His responses and salute to the Master's questions during the opening;

His responses and relevant salutes to the Junior Warden when opening the lodge into the higher degrees and closing down;

The correct introductions for latecomers, dignitaries and candidates;

The colloquies with the Tyler and Junior Warden/Master when candidates enter or re-enter the lodge room, and also the actions and when to perform them;

To wait for the Deacons to escort candidates, and possibly the Director of Ceremonies or Assistant Director of Ceremonies to escort latecomers and dignitaries;

When to pass any implement the Master may require during the ceremony;

The layout of the lighting switches if changes are required in the lodge room during the ceremonies;

How the door locks are operated, and when to open one or both doors for individuals or processions to enter or leave.

Deacons

Their places in opening and closing processions;

Their responses to the Master's questions during opening, if required;

Any formal opening of the VSL, lighting and extinguishing candles, etc., during the opening and closing;

How to deliver the Minute Book for signature;

How to conduct ballots, both by paper and balls;

How to escort dignitaries when required;

How to escort candidates around the lodge room;

The answers to the test questions when required;

How to demonstrate advancing to the East;

Where to place the candidate for the entrustings and explanations;

How to inform the candidate how to leave and enter the lodge room;

Where to sit the candidate when the ceremony is over.

Wardens

Their places in the opening and closing processions, as they may precede the Master in the first and follow him in the second;

Their parts in the opening and closing of all three degrees, and whether the closing will be in full or by virtue;

How to announce visitors, dignitaries and latecomers;

How to prove visitors in the three degrees, as appropriate for the meeting;

How the results of ballots are announced, and where to be and when, if appropriate;

What propositions they are expected to make or second (such as the formal acceptance of the Secretary's minutes, the Treasurer's accounts, etc.) and the correct words to be used;

Their roles in the ceremonies, especially when leaving their pedestals in the third degree and the actions they will undertake immediately afterwards;

When and when not to rise with the Master;

What toasts they are to propose at the festive board, how the names and offices are pronounced, and who the responders will be.

Master

Do I personally greet visitors going into the lodge room or after leaving?

What words are needed when welcoming brethren and opening the lodge;

When and how to offer the gavel of the lodge to the representative;

How to submit the minutes for confirmation, with or without the Wardens' proposing and seconding, and how to tell the Secretary his minutes are confirmed;

When to request a visiting dignitary or representative to countersign the minutes;

What words of congratulations to use to welcome joining members and candidates formally into what is now their lodge;

How to announce the risings, seated or standing;

With whom can I take wine without it becoming out of hand;

How to pronounce the items on the formal toast list, and especially what the initials stand for and which need to be read out loud;

With what words to close the festive board after the Tyler's toast.

Preparation of the Lodge Room

Primarily for the Tyler and Director of Ceremonies; but remember that, even with your best endeavours, you should request each Officer to check he has all of his required equipment for the business of the meeting, in order to avoid a temporary halt in the proceedings if a necessary item is missing at the appropriate juncture. Your lodge layout may contain the following:

At the Regular Officers' Stations:

Master's pedestal – has cushion, closed Book (with bookmarks), square and compasses, gavel, gauntlets, heavy maul and summons in place.

Senior Warden's pedestal – has cushion, Doric column – horizontal, gavel, gauntlets, level, summons.

Junior Warden's pedestal – has cushion, Corinthian column – vertical, gavel, gauntlets, plumb rule, summons.

Deacons' seats (and Director of Ceremonies' and Assistant Director of Ceremonies') – the correct holders for the respective wands are in place (and they may be of different diameters), and also the wands if appropriate.

Inner Guard's seat – has poignard or trowel, and square or compasses as appropriate, for use during the entry of the candidates.

Secretary's and Treasurer's table – spare summonses, lodge items, collection plates or bags, Minute Book, pedestal for reading, lodge bylaws, Book of Constitutions for reading of an ancient charge (if required) and regulations for the Master Elect at an installation or to give to candidates at their initiation, lodge ritual for reference and possible prompting, lodge memorabilia, etc.

Tyler's seat – has sword and summons, attendance register or sheet on a table adjacent to the entrance door together with a pen, and clothing for the candidate if required.

Other Equipment:

Ancient Charge or Book of Constitutions placed for whoever is reading an ancient charge during the opening of the meeting.

Ashlars to be placed appropriately; the rough one with the Junior Warden or in the North East corner of the square pavement; the perfect ashlar with the Senior Warden or in the South East corner, and the latter ashlar may be mounted on a tripod.

Banner displayed in lodge room, possibly also banners of lodges which have amalgamated with your lodge.

Candles to be checked they will light, with matches, taper or electricity as appropriate; place matches and taper ready for use (some lodges begin with candles already lit, others have a short ceremony to light them); if the candles are oil-fed, check there is enough oil for the meeting; if electric candles, check they are plugged in and that the bulbs work.

Hymn sheets on all seats or by entrance door (the Secretary, Treasurer and Organist will usually look after their own paperwork).

Officers' collars and aprons on appropriate seats or in the anteroom.

Pointer placed close by the tracing board to be explained, if required.

Rosettes (black), if it is traditional in the lodge for certain Officers to wear them if a member or a senior Provincial/Grand Officer has died.

Spare items, such as gloves, ties, aprons and collars if any member or visitor has forgotten them.

Tracing boards, if movable, placed appropriately round room and, even if nested together, ensure they are in the correct order.

Visitor cards will assist the Inner Guard to announce visitors and latecomers if the need arises, should be with the Tyler's book or signing-in sheets.

Wands to be placed in appropriate stands (check the sizes of the stands, as some wands may be of different diameter), or by the door of the lodge if it is customary to process in; doves, Mercuries or sun/moon for the Deacons and crossed wands for the Director of Ceremonies and Assistant Director of Ceremonies (in some lodges the Director of Ceremonies has a baton).

Warrant displayed in lodge room, or in a pouch for the Master (check it is the correct warrant), and any centenary or higher warrants, and also the warrants of lodges who may have amalgamated with yours.

Working tools placed appropriately for presentation.

Other Items:

Ballot box and balls – placed on Secretary's table if there is a ballot, and if necessary empty the drawer(s); paper slips if there is to be a written election.

Initiation – blindfold, cable tow and slipper near Tyler's seat; declaration book and collection plate at Secretary's table; Entered Apprentice apron at Master's or Senior Warden's pedestal; first degree tools at Master's or Junior Warden's pedestal; Book of Constitutions and lodge bylaws at the Master's pedestal.

Passing – slipper near Tyler's seat; square at Inner Guard's seat; Fellow Craft apron at Master's or Senior Warden's pedestal; second degree tools at Master's or Senior Warden's pedestal; floor cloth of a staircase if you have one.

Raising – 2 slippers near Tyler's seat; compasses at Inner Guard's seat; floor cloth and emblems of mortality for Deacons to lay out; torch for a Past Master to use; Master Mason apron at Master's or Senior Warden's pedestal (previously check for fit on candidate); third degree tools at Master's pedestal.

Installation – all sets of working tools and list of new Officers at Master's pedestal; Book of Constitutions and lodge bylaws at Secretary's table or appropriately placed; hanger or horse for Officers' collars when handed in; all collars to be worn or in the lodge room ready for investiture (to cover for absent brethren not able to hand in their collars).

Lectern – in position or ready to be moved into position if there is to be a lecture; often a job for the Assistant Director of Ceremonies, Deacons or Inner Guard.

Memorabilia – there may be items donated to the lodge by members or visitors that are to be displayed at meetings, for example on the Secretary's table, as well as other lodge furniture such as gongs, etc.

Mourning – pedestals and Secretary's table draped appropriately; black bows on columns and wands; black rosettes on Officers' collars and for other lodge members; a period of mourning may be decreed by Grand Lodge or Provincial Grand Lodge, or it may be caused by the death of a lodge member.

Ordering meals – count up the number of signatures in the Tyler's book, and check if the Director of Ceremonies has included the initiate(s) if it is a first degree ceremony.

Other Tyler's items – can include sticking plasters (to cover rings and earrings), stout rubber bands (in case the candidate's feet are much smaller than the slipshod), a torch if required in one of the ceremonies (and for power cuts), lighter or matches for the candles, as well as spare white gloves and black tie in case any visitor – and indeed any member - has forgotten these items, etc.

Processions Into and Out of the Lodge Room

If your lodge has a formal method of conducting the Master and his Wardens to their respective positions in the lodge room, the incoming procession may well include:

Assistant Director of Ceremonies   Director of Ceremonies
Tyler   Inner Guard
Junior Deacon   Senior Deacon

Other brethren as the traditions of the lodge dictate

Junior Warden   Senior Warden
Master

Chaplain   Immediate Past Master

It is noteworthy that the senior of two lodge Officers is on the right hand side of any pairing, and is therefore walking closest to the centre of the pavement, and this is a general principle adopted in most lodges. If your lodge invites visiting Masters, Grand and Provincial Grand Officers to join the inward procession, they will normally fit in behind the Director of Ceremonies or the Deacons, and then everyone stops and turns inwards to form a guard of honour for the Master to pass through into his chair. These additional members of the procession may be in order of seniority, juniors first, and they will find their seats around the East of the lodge room after the Master has taken his place. The Immediate Past Master and Chaplain will also stay in the East, leaving the remaining lodge Officers to escort the Wardens to their positions. The Junior Deacon will step into his place once the Senior Warden has arrived at his pedestal, the Tyler and Inner Guard will peel off to the door if that is situated in the North West, and the Senior Deacon will follow the Director of Ceremonies and his Assistant to his seat in the North East near to the Master. The Director of Ceremonies may lead the procession on his own, with his Assistant bringing up the rear; if this is the case, then the former may take his place after placing the Master in the East, and the Assistant attend to the other Principal Officers. In any event, the Director of Ceremonies with call the brethren already in the lodge room to order, "to receive the Worshipful Master, attended by his Wardens and accompanied by the Officers and … (whoever else is in the procession)", or words to that effect.

The retiring procession is almost the same, except that the Assistant Director of Ceremonies stands alone at the front while the Director of Ceremonies is escorting the various brethren to their places in the procession, and who normally remains in the lodge room as the procession exits. The Wardens will usually follow rather than precede the Master, as this time they are not forming a guard of honour as the junior Officers will do. Sometimes the Tyler and Inner Guard will collect the Wardens as they perambulate the lodge, and then wait in the North while the Director of Ceremonies arranges the rest of the procession before escorting the Master onto the floor of the lodge. Some lodges insist on placing every brother according to rank, while others invite selected brethren only, such as the representative at a meeting, the speaker, Grand Officers, visiting Masters (especially if a lodge is making a formal visit), and possibly the initiate, but each has its own traditions. The Deacons may cross their wands for brethren to pass underneath at both the incoming and outgoing processions and as the Wardens are escorted to their pedestals, whereas the Tyler and Inner Guard will find it more difficult to do so with their standard accoutrements.

List of Provincial Officers and Senior Grand Officers with Prefix and Salutes

Provincial Grand Officers Present and Past	Prefix	Salutes*
Deputy Provincial Grand Master	W.	5**
Assistant Provincial Grand Master	W.	5**
Senior Warden	W.	3
Junior Warden	W.	3
Chaplain	W.	3
Treasurer (elected, not appointed)	W.	3
Registrar	W.	3
Secretary	W.	3
Director of Ceremonies	W.	3
Sword Bearer	W.	3
Superintendent of Works	W.	3
Deputy Chaplain	W.	3
Deputy Registrar	W.	3
Deputy Secretary	W.	3
Deputy Director of Ceremonies	W.	3
Deputy Sword Bearer	W.	3
Deputy Superintendent of Works	W.	3
Almoner	W.	3
Charity Steward	W.	3
Senior Deacon	W.	3
Junior Deacon	W.	3
Assistant Chaplain	W.	3
Assistant Registrar	W.	3
Assistant Secretary	W.	3
Assistant Director of Ceremonies	W.	3
Assistant Sword Bearer	W.	3
Assistant Superintendent of Works	W.	3
Organist	W.	3
Standard Bearer	W.	3
Assistant Standard Bearer	W.	3

Deputy Organist	W.	3
Pursuivant	W.	3
Assistant Pursuivant	W.	3
Steward	W.	3
Tyler	W.	3

Senior Grand Officers Present and Past	**Prefix**	**Salutes**
Grand Master	M.W.	11
Pro Grand Master	M.W.	11
Deputy Grand Master	R.W.	7
Assistant Grand Master	R.W.	7
Grand Wardens	R.W.	7
Provincial Grand Master	R.W.	7
Pro Provincial Grand Master	R.W.	7
Grand Chaplain	V.W.	5
Grand Sword Bearer	V.W.	5
Grand Superintendent of Works	V.W.	5
Grand Senior Deacon	W.	3
Grand Junior Deacon	W.	3
All Other Grand Officers	W.	3

* In their own Province only
** Deputy and Assistant Provincial Grand Masters receive a salute of five if they have held the office for more than 2 years (BoC 6)

Formal Seating Plan for Meals

If there is a top table, the Master is seated centrally; next to him on his right hand are:

Initiate;
Provincial Grand Master or his representative;
Grand Officers in descending order of seniority (and by year of appointment);
Senior guests.

And on his left hand are:

Immediate Past Master;
Chaplain;
Treasurer;
Secretary;
Director of Ceremonies;
Past Masters of the lodge in order of seniority.

The Wardens may be seated at the ends of the top table, or at the ends of the outermost sprig tables, depending on lodge custom and practice.

The Master's personal guests may be seated in front of him on an adjacent sprig table, so that he has the opportunity to converse with them during the meal.

If there is music or the Master's song is to be sung during or after the meal, it is likely that the brethren involved will want to sit together, to make any last-minute musical arrangements, and the pianist will probably prefer to be seated near to the piano.

Some senior attendees, which may include Grand Officers (sometimes referred to as Officers of Grand Lodge, but please not Grand Lodge Officers – unless one happens to be an active Grand Officer of the year), may request to be seated elsewhere in the table plan, perhaps to be near other guests who cannot be placed adjacent to the top table for them to converse with. You might even invite them to consider doing this occasionally, so that they can mix with the other ranks of Masons present; it has a remarkably encouraging effect if junior brethren realise they are sitting and talking with senior brethren, and each can usefully learn informally from the other which they might not otherwise be able to do if the seating plans always follow a strict hierarchical order.

Taking Wine and Formal Toasts

Taking Wine

The taking of wine with the brethren can be fraught with difficulties. Too little will leave some attendees feeling overlooked, and too much of a good thing will potentially spoil the proceedings for everyone. One good rule of thumb is not to take wine with anybody who is going to be the recipient of a toast later in the evening. It is unnecessary to interrupt every course of the meal by taking wine, so try to complete the necessary items in perhaps one or two sessions, and then the diners can continue their meals in peace.

As a way of introducing some variety into your preamble to take wine, you may say that the Master:

> now wishes, has expressed the wish/desire,
> will take great/particular pleasure,
> is delighted and honoured, is equally delighted,
> is now eager/anxious, is now proud and happy.

The following list may be of assistance to the Master as he takes wine with the:

Wardens (particularly if they join in with the Master in subsequent toasts)**
Provincial Grand Master or representative
(he may then take wine with everyone else)
Visiting Masters
A brother on a special celebration, e.g. 50th anniversary of Initiation
Officers and members of the lodge who participated in the ceremony
Candidate (Fellowcraft, Master Mason but not Initiate)
Joining members
Master Elect
New lodge Officers
Founders or Past Masters of the lodge
Personal guests
Other (or all) members of the lodge
Other (or all) visiting brethren
Any brother with whom he has not yet taken wine (an alternative catch-all)

** The Master, Immediate Past Master, or Director of Ceremonies may introduce this by using part of the long Tyler's toast along these lines:

Master – Brother Wardens, how do you report your respective stations?
Senior Warden – The glasses are fully charged in the West.
Junior Warden – The glasses are fully charged in the South.
Master – And I report the same for the East and North; Brother
       Wardens, I have much pleasure in taking wine with you both.

Toasts

The following is a generally accepted generic set of toasts to be used on formal occasions, but each Province will provide a detailed Toast List to be used within the Province:

The Queen and the Craft

Grand Master

Pro Grand Master
Deputy Grand Master
Assistant Grand Master
and the rest of the Grand Officers, present and past

Provincial Grand Master

Deputy Provincial Grand Master
Assistant Provincial Grand Master(s)
and the rest of the Provincial Grand Officers, present and past, of this and other Provinces, and holders of Metropolitan and London Grand Rank

Master

Initiate

Visitors

Tyler's

Additional toasts may also be included as required, such as:

Immediate Past (and Installing) Master; Installation team; Masonic charities; Absent brethren (if referred to as the 9 o'clock toast – when the hands of the clock are at the square - it should be honoured at 9pm; if simply designated to absent brethren, this can be taken at any time); Founders of the lodge; Tyler's toast (may be the long version at an installation, Olde English Night or other special occasion)

––––––––––––––––

The charity collection, taken in lodge or at the festive board, may be announced by the Master before or during his closing remarks. If the lodge responds to the toasts using firing glasses, then there is usually no fire after absent brethren if it precedes the loyal toast (which preferably it does not), after Masonic charities, or after the Tyler's toast, or there may be 'silent fire'. Some lodges adopt 'silent fire' and others deprecate it, but your visitors should be courteous and "when in Rome…"

––––––––––––––––

Serenity for Directors of Ceremonies

Grant me the serenity to accept the things I cannot change;
the courage to change the things I cannot accept;
and the wisdom to hide the bodies of those I had to kill today,
because they got on my nerves.
Also help me to be careful of the toes I step on today,
as they may be connected to the feet I have to kiss tomorrow.
And help me to remember that when I am having a bad day,
and it seems that people are trying to wind me up,
it takes 42 muscles to frown,
but only 28 to smile.

About the Author

Richard Johnson graduated from Cambridge University in 1967 with a BA honours in Natural Sciences and Metallurgy, and received his MA in 1970; and then was awarded a PhD from Surrey University in 1974 in Materials Science and Metallurgy – all degrees associated with being an 'artificer in metals'.

He was initiated into Salwick Lodge 7993 of Preston and West Lancashire in January 1983, and became Master in November 1992, and was promoted to Past Provincial Junior Grand Deacon in West Lancashire in May 1998. He later joined Isaac Newton University Lodge 859 of Cambridge in June 1999 and the Blackburn Lodge of Masonic Research 6720 of Darwen and East Lancashire in January 2001. Later he joined Lodge of Unanimity 113 of Preston in November 2007, and became Master in 2009.

In March 2001 he became the founding Master of Brigantes Lodge 9734 of Kendal and Cumberland & Westmorland, a lodge created by keen ritualists to perform the long versions of each of the ceremonies – including some of the rarely used items at the backs of the ritual books. In agreeing on the methodology to be adopted in the new lodge, he led some lively discussions about the Craft ritual in a working party, and retains a keen interest in all of the traditional aspects of lodge workings, especially in learning of any unusual ceremonial that exist. He was appointed to Past Provincial Senior Grand Deacon in this Province in October 2003. He also leads the lodge demonstration team, re-enacting lodge ceremonies from the eighteenth century workings, for the enjoyment (and possibly education) of host lodges and their guests, and all to raise money for charity.

He has given invited lectures on the development of the early lodges in Lancashire, Cumberland & Westmorland and the North West in general. In December 1999 he published a book, *Preston Radiant*, on the history of the thirty-six lodges in that town and also covering several of the surrounding lodges in the North West, from their warranting by the different Grand Lodges to the end of the second millennium. Since then he has written books containing practical advice for the lodge Officers, this one being the sixth in the series.

This book is part of a series of books for lodge Officers:
The Assistant Officers – a Practical Guide;
The Principal Officers – a Practical Guide;
The Secretary and Director of Ceremonies – a Practical Guide;
The Treasurer, Charity Steward and Almoner – a Practical Guide;
The Lodge Mentor.

The Director of Ceremonies